THE PEOPLE OF ANCIENT ISRAEL

THE PEOPLE OF ANCIENT ISRAEL

BY

DOROTHY MILLS

Angelico Press, 2012
First edition, Charles Scribner's Sons, 1932

For information, address:
Angelico Press, 4619 Slayden Rd., NE
Tacoma, WA 98422
www.angelicopress.com

Library of Congress Cataloging-in-Publication Data

Mills, Dorothy.
The people of ancient Israel / by Dorothy Mills.

p. cm.
Originally published: [New York]: C. Scribner's sons, 1932.
Includes index.
ISBN 978-1-59731-355-1 (pbk.: alk. paper)
ISBN 978-1-59731-380-3 (hardback: alk. paper)
1. Jews—History—To 70 A.D. 2. Bible. O.T.—History of Biblical events.
3. Bible—History of Biblical events. I. Title.
DS118.M66 2008
933—dc22 2008023148

Jacket Design: Michael Schrauzer

TO

W. F. W.

ACKNOWLEDGMENTS

In *The Book of the Ancient World,* published by Messrs. G. P. Putnam's Sons in 1923, the story of the peoples of ancient civilisation, one section of the book was devoted to the Hebrews. This section has been drawn upon liberally, and I wish to acknowledge here the courtesy of the publishers in permitting me to do so.

Acknowledgment is made to The Macmillan Company, publishers, for permission to arrange selections from the Psalms as they appear in Moulton's *The Modern Reader's Bible,* and to arrange Psalm XXIV as it appears in *The Psalms* by Four Friends; also to the Oxford University Press for arrangement of selections taken from the Prophets as they appear in Woods and Powell's *The Hebrew Prophets.* In these instances, however, the text of the King James Version has been followed.

For beauty of language and nobility of style the Authorised or King James Version of the Bible has never been surpassed and Biblical quotations that occur in this book have been taken from that translation, except for a few instances where the Revised Version has been used and is indicated.

PREFACE

The history of the people of ancient Israel is as interesting as any in the world. The stories of its heroes, its poets and prophets, mighty men of valour and famous women are found in a literature which has been a source of interest and inspiration throughout the ages. The history of this people centres round the story of their search to know the character of God, and the literature they have given to the world has made a lasting contribution to the spiritual life of man.

This book presents in brief form the record of the Hebrew people from their earliest times to the destruction of Jerusalem in A.D. 70. It shows the Hebrews not only developing their own civilisation with emphasis on their social life and customs, it also shows them in their relation to other nations of the ancient world, and above all it stresses the development of the idea of God in the Hebrew mind.

This book is the outcome of my experience in teaching the history of the ancient world to young people. I hope that readers as they turn these pages will also follow what the Hebrews themselves wrote in that great book which we call the Bible.

DOROTHY MILLS.

NEW YORK,
January, 1932.

CONTENTS

CHAPTER		PAGE
I.	The Land of Palestine	1
II.	The Hebrew Scriptures	4
III.	Early Hebrew Tales	6
	THE CREATION OF THE WORLD	7
	THE GARDEN OF EDEN	8
	CAIN AND ABEL	9
	THE FLOOD	11
	THE TOWER OF BABEL	12
IV.	The Founders of the Hebrew Nation	14
	CANAAN IN THE AGE OF THE PATRIARCHS	14
	THE PATRIARCHS IN CANAAN	17
	ABRAHAM AND ISAAC	17
	JACOB	24
	THE STORY OF JOSEPH	30
V.	Moses and the Exodus from Egypt	33
VI.	The Making of the Hebrew Nation	39
	THE GIVING OF THE LAW	39
	LIFE IN THE WILDERNESS	44
VII.	The Conquest of Canaan and the Age of the Judges	51
	THE TAKING OF THE LAND	51
	CUSTOMS IN EARLY ISRAEL	55
	JUDGES IN ISRAEL	58
	SAMSON, THE STRONG MAN	62
	THE STORY OF RUTH	64
	SAMUEL, THE LAST JUDGE	65

CHAPTER PAGE

VIII. The United Kingdom of Israel 70
SAUL, THE WARRIOR 70
SAUL AND DAVID 73
DAVID, THE HERO-KING OF ISRAEL 79
SOLOMON, THE BUILDER 86

IX. Rebellion and the Division of the Kingdom 90

X. How Men Lived in Israel Under the Kings 93

XI. Kings in Israel from Jeroboam to Jehu 102

XII. The Hebrew Prophet 111
THE PROPHET 111
THE FORERUNNERS: ELIJAH AND ELISHA . 113

XIII. The Fall of Northern Israel 117
THE PROPHETS: AMOS AND HOSEA . . . 117
THE FALL OF SAMARIA 123

XIV. The Kingdom of Judah 125
KINGS OF THE HOUSE OF DAVID 125
ISAIAH, THE STATESMAN-PROPHET . . . 131

XV. The Fall of Judah 138
THE REFORMATION UNDER JOSIAH . . . 138
JEREMIAH, THE PERSECUTED PROPHET . . 141
THE FALL OF JERUSALEM 145

XVI. In Captivity 146

XVII. The Return from Exile 153
THE REBUILDING OF JERUSALEM . . . 153
THE UNKNOWN PROPHET 157
JERUSALEM UNDER THE HIGH PRIESTS . . 164

CHAPTER PAGE

XVIII. Israel Under the Greeks and Romans . 169
THE HELLENISTIC PERIOD 169
THE MACCABEES 173
THE ROMANS AND THE DESTRUCTION OF JERUSALEM 175

Reference List of Bible Stories . . . 181

Suggestions About Books for Further Reading 187

Index 189

MAPS AND CHARTS

PAGE

Mesopotamia in Ancient Times 19
The United Kingdom of Israel 71
Chart I: 30th Through 10th Century, B.C. . . 91
Chart II: 9th Through 6th Century, B.C. . . 147
Chart III: 5th Through A.D. 70 167

THE PEOPLE
OF ANCIENT ISRAEL

THE PEOPLE OF ANCIENT ISRAEL

CHAPTER I

THE LAND OF PALESTINE

PALESTINE is a little land. Some little lands have been of great importance in history; for instance, Greece, England, Belgium, and Palestine itself. The Palestine of the Hebrews was situated between the lands where the great empires of Egypt and Assyria and Babylon flourished. She was a bridge between Africa and Asia, the meeting place for travellers between these lands, and in consequence the civilisation of these places passed through her. But just as in modern times Belgium, being on one of the highroads between France and Germany, has been used as a battlefield by European nations, so in ancient times Palestine, on the highroad between Egypt and Babylon, was also a battlefield. This was especially true of the north, in the Plain of Jezreel or Megiddo. The war and commerce of nearly all the ancient world passed through this land.

The coast line of Palestine had only one or two good harbours, but these were in the north and belonged to the Phœnicians. The Hebrew inhabitants of Palestine were not sailors. They looked upon the sea as a boundary, as something that cut them off from other peoples; it was never a highway to them.

The climate of Palestine is varied. The top of Mount Hermon is covered with snow, but not far off is the valley of the Jordan with its palm trees and tropical plants. In ancient times there was more forest land than now—cedar, cypress, oak, sycamore and acacia trees. In those days there were more olives, and there were "terraces clad with vines."

There are two clearly marked seasons in Palestine, the rainy and the dry. The rains fall from October to April, the *early* or the *former* rains at the end of October, and the *latter* rains in March and April. These *latter* rains are heavy and of great importance. They are the last rains before the long summer drought and the harvest depends upon them. From May to October the land is dry.

Spring is very beautiful in Palestine, for the countryside is full of wild flowers. The Hebrews called this season the time of the "coming of flowers," and one of their poets wrote of the spring:

> Lo, the winter is past,
> The rain is over and gone;
> The flowers appear on the earth;
> The time of the singing of birds is come,
> And the voice of the turtle is heard in our land;
> The fig tree ripeneth her green figs,
> And the vines are in blossom,
> They give forth their fragrance.[1]

During the dry season there was often a scarcity of water, the wells and brooks dried up, and at

[1]Song of Songs, ii, 12–13, R. V.

times water had even to be bought. This accounts for the frequent mention by Hebrew writers of springs of water and the importance they attached to wells. In the language of poetry, which is one of the characteristics of Hebrew literature, those whose lives are guided by the grace of God are compared to a "watered garden, and like a spring of water, whose waters fail not."

The Hebrew people who came to this land and settled in it lived originally beyond the Euphrates, and the word "Hebrew" means a "dweller on the other side." The Hebrews called themselves the "Sons of Israel," taking their name from one of their ancestors. It is the story of these people that we read about in the Bible.

CHAPTER II

THE HEBREW SCRIPTURES

The world owes a great deal to the Egyptians and Babylonians, but it owes still more to the Hebrews, for it was they who taught the world the knowledge of God. Politically the Hebrews were of little account in the world, but, in the story of man's learning how to live and his search to satisfy the longings of his spirit, they stand supreme.

The history of the Hebrews is found in that part of the Bible known as the Old Testament. The word "Bible" is derived from a Greek word meaning "books," and the Bible is made up of many different books, written by different writers over a long period of years. At one time it was called the "Divine Library," a name which well describes it, for the Bible contains the literature of the Hebrew people: their legends and poetry, religious teaching, history and law.

The Bible was not written down in the form in which we have it until many centuries after the events which the history records had taken place. There were older records, some of them written, some of them traditions which had been handed down by word of mouth for many ages, hero stories and ancient hymns of the Hebrew race. At length this scattered material was put together and formed the Hebrew Scriptures.

These writings are interesting records of progress, from ignorance to fuller knowledge, and from lower to higher ideals. Religion held the most important place in the minds of the writers, and the history of the Hebrew people is chiefly the history of how they learned to know the character of God. He was known to them at first by a Name so holy that it was rarely spoken. In reading when they came to it, they said simply, LORD. Later translators of the Bible have used the name JEHOVAH.

In the beginning the Hebrews thought of Jehovah as a stern master whose anger had to be appeased. Later, He was to them the Lord of Hosts, who fought for them as their Leader in war. At this time they believed that other nations had other gods, but they were different from Jehovah, for these gods were not regarded, even by those who believed in them, as entirely free from human frailties, whereas Jehovah was a God of absolute righteousness and justice. As the centuries went by, the Hebrews learned that their early conceptions of Jehovah were inadequate. They learned that He was the One God of the whole world. Through their experiences they discovered that:

Jehovah hath showed thee, O man, what is good;
And what doth He require of thee,
    But to do justly,
    And to love mercy,
    And to walk humbly with thy God?[1]

[1]Micah vi, 8.

CHAPTER III

EARLY HEBREW TALES

THE ancient Hebrew historian thought of the history of his race as a drama, the story of which was the relation between Jehovah and man. This drama was to have in it a great tragedy, but the Hebrew was to learn, as all nations and individuals have learnt at some time or other, that true greatness is born of suffering and sacrifice. There was to come a time in the story of the Hebrew nation when one of their leaders cried out: "Zion is taken from us, nothing is left save the Holy One and His Law." It was true; nothing material had been left them. As a nation they were conquered and cast out into exile, yet the greatest thing they possessed, the priceless gift they had for the world was not taken from them. Out of the tragedy they were to learn that the Holy One and His Law is eternal.

The opening chapters of the book of Genesis are the prologue to this story. In them are set forth certain great truths. The Hebrews were an eastern people. Like other eastern peoples they used a language of poetry, and one of their favourite ways of teaching a lesson was by means of a parable. *A truth* is not the same thing as *the truth,* and the Hebrews are not the only people who have used myths, allegories, parables or fairy-tales as the setting for some teaching. Primitive peoples asked the same questions that great philosophers asked later, and many of the questions have not yet been answered, for an answer that satisfies one generation does not always satisfy the next. Increased knowledge sometimes makes earlier answers, if not wrong, at least inadequate. No one answer given by man contains the whole truth, for the human mind is finite and cannot see all sides at once, but whatever form the answer may take, if it is a sincere answer based on sound knowledge, it contains some portion of the underlying truth which is eternal.

The Creation of the World

One of the oldest of the questions asked and asked again was: How was the world made? How were men and women made? How were all living things made?

Now the Hebrew was not concerned with what science had to teach. In the far-off days when he sought an answer to this question, the scientific knowledge in the world was very small, was inaccurate and inadequate and very much mixed up with superstition. The Hebrew did not even know much of what science there was, but he believed one thing: that behind everything was a Creator and Ruler of the universe, whose will it was that nature should work by means of law and order, and that this law and order should minister to the happiness and well-being of man. The Hebrew writer framed these great truths in the story of the Creation.

In the beginning, we are told, God created the

heavens and the earth. Over the darkness which lay on the face of the great formless deep, the Spirit of God moved, and God created the light. He made the day and the night, and heaven and earth; and the earth was made fruitful and the sun and the moon and the stars gave light to it. Living creatures were created, the fish in the sea, and birds of the air, and cattle and beasts on the earth. And then God created Man that he might rule over all that He had made, and the story tells us that God saw everything that He had made, and behold, it was very good. And God rested from His work, and the day on which He rested was set apart and blessed and sanctified.

The Garden of Eden

"And God saw everything that He had made, and behold, it was very good." Yet as soon as man began to think much about the world, he saw a great deal in it that was not good. He saw injustice, dishonesty, and all kinds of wrong-doing, and he asked the question that is still being asked: What is sin and evil and where does it come from? All kinds of answers have been and are still being given to this question, but the same truth is found in all: that sin is disobedience to some kind of law, that sin creates a barrier between the sinner and the sinned against, and that sin brings with it consequences that cannot be avoided. The Hebrew teachers had a passionate belief in the absolute purity and righteousness of God, and they enshrined their teaching of what they believed sin was and of all that it brought with it in the story of Adam and Eve in the Garden of Eden.

The garden was fragrant with flowers, well watered and rich in trees that were both pleasant to the sight and good for food. Adam and Eve were brought to the garden and told that it was theirs to care for and to cultivate. They might eat of the fruit of all the trees save one, and that was the tree of the knowledge of good and evil. Of the fruit of that tree they were never to eat.

Adam and Eve dwelt happily in the garden. But one day Eve was assailed by temptation in the form of a serpent, who prevailed upon her to taste the fruit of the forbidden tree, and she tasted it and gave some to Adam. That evening Adam and Eve knew that their act of disobedience had destroyed the old simplicity of their relations with the Lord. It was His custom to walk in the garden in the cool of the day and Adam and Eve would walk with Him. But this evening, for the first time, they were afraid and hid themselves in the trees of the garden. Not until they were called did they appear, and then they had to confess what they had done. For their disobedience they were turned out of the garden to till the ground outside, and the entrance of the garden was guarded by cherubim with a flaming sword.

Cain and Abel

Driven out of the Garden of Eden, Adam and Eve found a new home for themselves, and soon after, we are told that Cain and Abel were born.

Abel was a shepherd and Cain a farmer, and they brought their offerings to the Lord, the one of his flock and the other from his fields. The offering of Abel was accepted, but that of Cain seems to have been rejected. No reason is given but it would seem from the old Hebrew story that Abel had brought an offering that cost him something, for we are told that it was of the "firstlings of his flock," the best that he had, whereas of Cain, we are only told that he brought of the fruit of the ground, an offering that probably cost him nothing and was merely an outward form.

Jealousy of his brother seized hold of the heart of Cain, and meeting Abel in the field, he slew him. But Abel was his brother, and when Cain heard the question, "Where is Abel thy brother?" he replied in angry shame, "I know not: am I my brother's keeper?" Then the voice of God told him that he was, and that as a punishment he was to be driven out from his home and lose, in consequence, the tribal protection that was so essential to safety amongst the nomads of the East. And Cain went out, a fugitive and a vagabond in the earth.

This story is followed by a list of the descendants of Adam and Eve down to the time of Noah. There are a number of such genealogical lists in the Bible, and scattered through them are here and there allusions which tell something of ancient Hebrew life, or a sentence or two that reveal some personality that for various reasons stood out from the others and was specially remembered in his family. These allusions are like sudden flashes of light in a dark place.

In this list we hear of Jabal who was called "the father of such as dwell in tents and of such as have cattle," of his brother Jubal, "the father of all such as handle the harp and organ," and of Tubal-Cain, "an instructor of every artificer in brass and iron." We read of Enoch, who "walked with God, and was not, for God took him," and of his son Methuselah, the oldest man who ever lived, for he was said to have been nine hundred and sixty-nine years old when he died.

The Flood

Most primitive people had amongst their earliest traditions the story of a great flood. The Hebrew story closely resembles that of the Babylonians. Men had multiplied upon the earth, they had become powerful, they gloried in their strength, and in their pride they forgot Jehovah. There were "giants in the earth in those days, and their children became mighty men which were of old, men of renown." There were men like Nimrod, the hunter, who was a mighty man in the earth.

The ancient tale tells us that because men trusted in themselves, and because the thoughts of their hearts had grown evil and worldly, the Lord repented that He had made man and determined to destroy him. But one man had found grace in His sight, Noah, and he and his family were to be saved.

Noah was told to build an ark and to take into it his wife, his three sons and their wives, and two of every beast of the field and bird of the air. He did this, and for forty days a flood came upon the face of the earth and everything living on the earth died. But Noah and his ark floated on the top of the waters, until at length it rested on Mount Ararat. At the end of forty days, Noah opened the window of the ark and sent out two birds, a raven and a dove. The raven did not return. It went to and fro until dry land appeared again, but the dove, finding no rest for the sole of her foot came back to the ark, where Noah kept her for seven days and then sent her out again. This time she returned with an olive leaf in her mouth. Noah kept her yet another seven days, and then once more sent her out. This time she did not return, so Noah knew that the earth was dry again.

Then Noah went out of the ark and built an altar to Jehovah and offered a thanksgiving for his preservation. Jehovah accepted his worship and promised that never again should the whole earth be destroyed by a flood. And as an outward token of His promise, He set a rainbow in the sky.

The Tower of Babel

These early chapters contain one more ancient story. It contains a truth more often forgotten than remembered in history, the truth that in spite of differences of environment, of race, or of language, the whole world is one family in its relation to God.

The story relates that in the dawn of the world the whole earth spoke one language. In order to bind themselves more closely together, the men of those days determined to build a tower, the top of which should reach to heaven. But Jehovah did not allow them to finish, for He regarded the tower as a symbol of the arrogance of men who were trying to make themselves the equals of God. He went down to earth, and confused their speech, so that they no longer understood each other. Then He scattered them abroad over the face of the earth. The name given to the tower they tried to build was Babel, because of the confusion that had been created in that place, but the people who were scattered and who now spoke different languages, had once been one people bound together by race and language.

With this story the prologue to the history ends, and we come to the story of Abraham, the traditional founder of the Hebrew nation.

CHAPTER IV

THE FOUNDERS OF THE HEBREW NATION

Canaan in the Age of the Patriarchs

It was in the days of Abraham that the Hebrews first entered Canaan. The Hebrews were nomads, people with no definite home, but the Canaanites had passed from that stage of living and were more settled, living for the most part in walled towns set on the hilltops. These towns were grouped together in small independent city-principalities, ruled by native princes who called themselves kings. These kings were constantly fighting amongst themselves, always afraid of the Hittites to the north of them and keeping the peace with Egypt by paying heavy tribute to the Pharaoh. The Canaanites were a civilised people, skilled in many arts, and they were evidently rich and prosperous. A list of the booty taken from them by Thutmose III at Megiddo shows the kind of possessions they had at that time. (This list is inscribed on the temple built by Thutmose III at Thebes, and recent excavations in Palestine have shown it to be an accurate one.) The booty consisted of chariots and weapons of all kinds, coats of mail, and a goodly collection of furniture that had belonged to the King of Kadesh: beds and tables of costly woods inlaid with gold and precious stones, vessels of bronze and gold, drinking-cups, bowls and jars of rare Syrian workmanship.

The Canaanite kings were evidently familiar with the Babylonian script, the script of diplomacy of the ancient world, for some of the Tell-el-Amarna Letters are part of a correspondence between the King of Egypt and certain Canaanite rulers.

The religion of this people was a nature religion, and the chief feasts were those connected in various ways with the agricultural life of the land. Every region had its own god, who was looked upon as the owner of all the gifts of nature. The general name for the chief Canaanite god was Baal, and he was worshipped in many holy places: in fountains and springs of water, under groves of trees, in sanctuaries on "every high hill and under every green tree." These sacred places were often marked by a stone pillar or an altar, where offerings were presented and sacrifices made. Amongst the Canaanites human sacrifices were not unknown.

Into this land came the Hebrews. These early Hebrews were shepherds, and like all shepherd peoples of the ancient world, they were nomads, wandering from place to place in search of different oases where they might feed and water their flocks. They were not unlike the more modern Bedouin. Their flocks were chiefly of sheep and goats, and they used camels instead of horses. For clothing they wore a long under-garment, with a cloak, a turban and sandals. Their food was chiefly milk, butter, dates, meal and oil.

The Bedouin himself is aristocratic. His wandering life prevents him from having a settled home, inherited from his ancestors, and in its stead he glories in his lineage. But the organisation of Bedouin life is democratic. The loyalty of a tribesman to his chief is the loyalty and devotion of comrades who are equals. The head of the tribe is the man to whom the tribe gives the greatest respect, but he keeps his position only as long as his will is also the will of the tribe. To the nomad, belonging to a tribe was essential. A place in a tribe was his home, and to be outside meant that he was homeless, that he had no protection during life and no one to avenge him did he meet with a violent death. It was this fate that was so appalling to Cain. "Behold, thou hast driven me out this day from the face of the earth; and from thy face shall I be hid; and I shall be a fugitive and a vagabond in the earth; and it shall come to pass, that every one that findeth me shall slay me."[1]

The early Bedouin life must once have been something like that of the wild ass described by Job.

> Who hath sent out the wild ass free?
> Or who hath loosed the bands of the wild ass?
> Whose house I have made the wilderness,
> And the barren land his dwelling.
> He scorneth the tumult of the city,
> Neither heareth he the shoutings of the driver.
> The range of the mountains is his pasture,
> And he searcheth after every green thing.[2]

The life of these earliest Bedouins was a hard one. They built no house, sowed no seed, planted no

[1]Genesis iv, 14.
[2]Job xxxix, 5–8.

vineyard, drank no wine. Yet long years after the days of the Patriarchs, when Hebrew life had become more settled and people were building cities, men looked to the old nomad days as to a period when ideals were high and life was simple, lived in clearer realisation of the presence of Jehovah. Attempts were made to preserve these old ideals by groups of people who banded themselves together in a kind of brotherhood, some calling themselves Nazirites and others Rechabites, after the name of their founder. "We will drink no wine," they said, "for Jonadab the son of Rechab our father commanded us, saying, Ye shall drink no wine, neither ye, nor your sons for ever; neither shall ye build houses, nor sow seed, nor plant vineyard, nor have any: but all your days ye shall dwell in tents; that ye may live many days in the land where ye be strangers."[1]

The early Patriarchs were Bedouins from the desert lands, nomads with their flocks and herds, and it was this life that they brought with them into Canaan.

The Patriarchs in Canaan

ABRAHAM AND ISAAC

The Hebrews lived originally near the banks of the Euphrates. We are told that the patriarch Abraham who lived in Haran, but who had come earlier from Ur of the Chaldees, a rich man owning flocks and herds, received a call that he recognised

[1]Jeremiah xxxv, 6–7.

as coming from Jehovah. The call urged him to leave his home and friends and kindred, and to travel west to a new home in the land then known as Canaan. With the call was a promise that he should become the father of a great nation, and that his descendants should possess the land to which he was to journey.

It was not an unknown thing for a man such as Abraham to seek a new home, where perhaps the pasture would be better, and the springs of water more conveniently situated. But Abraham was to go a much further distance than such journeys generally took men, and he must have been very full of a spirit of adventure and of sure faith in the outcome to have started.

Now Abraham was very rich in cattle, in silver and in gold, and Lot, his nephew who accompanied him, was also a rich man having many flocks and herds and tents. As they drew near the land of Canaan, the company was too large to keep together, for at the oases where they stopped for pasture and water, the shepherds of Abraham quarrelled with those of Lot over the best sites for their flocks. The result was that Abraham proposed to Lot that they should separate and he gave Lot the choice of the direction in which he would go. Lot chose the well-watered plain of the Jordan and they parted, Abraham moving his tents to the neighbourhood of Hebron.

Not long after the separation of Abraham and Lot a war broke out in Canaan. Four kings and their armies fought against five other kings and

MESOPOTAMIA
in ancient
times
100 MILES
ASIA MINOR
Caspian Sea
Grazing land
Nineveh
Medes
ASSYRIA
SYRIA
Euphrates
Tigris
Fertile land
The Army
MEDITERRANEAN
Tyre
Lebanon
Damascus
Babylon
Chaldeans
Persians
Desert
BABYLONIA
Susa
Hebrews
Jerusalem
Dead Sea
The present bed
of the Euphrates
Ur
Persian Gulf
The present shore
of the Persian Gulf
EGYPT
Red Sea
RAISZ

their armies, and amongst the latter was the King of Sodom. The five kings were defeated and they fled to the mountains for refuge. Their enemies took all the spoil left on the battlefield and a great many prisoners, amongst whom was Lot who had made his home in the city of Sodom. The news of this battle and of the capture of Lot soon reached Abraham, who immediately summoned his servants, trained like all Bedouin herdsmen to fight when necessary, and they rescued Lot and his possessions. Lot returned to Sodom and Abraham went with his flocks and herds to the plains of Mamre. On his way he was met by Melchizedek, King of Salem, who brought him bread and wine, and blessed him, saying: "Blessed be Abraham of the most high God, possessor of heaven and earth: And blessed be the most high God, which hath delivered thine enemies into thine hand."[1]

One of the strongest traditions of the Bedouin was that of hospitality, and it was while Abraham was in the plains of Mamre that he entertained three men whom he recognised later as men who had come to him with a special message from Jehovah. Life in the wide and silent spaciousness of the desert had brought the world of the spirit very near to Abraham and his spiritual hearing was very quick to discern the voice of God speaking to him in whatever form it might come. The story of Abraham and these men is full of the courtesy of desert hospitality. Water was brought to wash their feet, hot and dusty from the journey; bread, meat and

[1]Genesis xiv, 19–20.

milk of the best was set before them that they might eat and drink. Then, refreshed with the food and milk, they told Abraham that God would give him and Sarah, his wife, a son whose descendants should inherit the land where he dwelt. Then they rose up to leave him. As they went, they looked towards Sodom, and Abraham went with them for a part of the way.

It must be remembered that the stories told us in the book of Genesis were written down long after the events narrated had taken place, and that in interpreting their history the Hebrew writers were concerned mainly with one idea, the righteousness of Jehovah in His dealings with His people, and the belief that wrath and destruction awaited all those who did not acknowledge Him as God. The Hebrews of the Old Testament were people of their time, and they shared with other eastern peoples the belief that disaster and destruction were signs of punishment for evil-doing, and so when the cities of Sodom and Gomorrah were destroyed by an earthquake, they did not hesitate in attributing the disaster to the wickedness of the inhabitants. Lot, we are told, escaped, not because he himself was righteous—the story never shows Lot in a particularly favourable light—but because he was loved by Abraham, the man whom later ages loved to describe as the "friend of God."

Not long afterwards a son was born to Abraham and Sarah, and Abraham called him Isaac. It was the custom in the ancient East for a man to have more than one wife and besides Sarah, Abraham had a wife, Hagar, who had been an Egyptian slave. Hagar had a son Ishmael, of whom it was said that he would be "a wild man, that his hand would be against every man and every man's hand against him." Sarah was jealous of Ishmael, and when Isaac was born she did not like the thought that her son might have to share his inheritance with the son of an Egyptian bondwoman, whom she despised. In order that Isaac might grow up as the recognised heir of his father's wealth, she meanly persuaded Abraham to send Hagar and Ishmael away. They were sent off, but we are told that the lad grew and became a good archer. When he was a man he became the head of a desert tribe, and it is thought by some scholars that he may have been the ancestor of the modern Arab.

Now it was a very early belief amongst all eastern nations that to offer one's dearest possessions as a sacrifice to God was something especially well pleasing to Him, and they believed that blood, without which no man could live was the most valuable thing that could be offered. From this belief came the custom, that was especially prevalent in Canaan, of making human sacrifices.

It was not surprising, therefore, that the idea came to Abraham that it would be well pleasing to Jehovah if he offered to Him as a sacrifice Isaac, his best beloved son. All his hopes for his race centred in Isaac, but once he had convinced himself that the sacrifice was demanded of him by Jehovah Himself, he prepared to carry it out unflinchingly. One of the characteristics of the Hebrew writers is their simplicity in telling a story. They do not describe the feelings and emotions of the people about whom they are writing, but the very simplicity of the outward form leaves the imagination free to picture the scene and to understand all that it meant. We see Abraham going off with Isaac and two servants up into the hill-country, well away from his tents and shepherds, well away from Sarah, answering the questions of Isaac shortly, at the last moment going on alone with Isaac, and in silence building an altar and making ready to sacrifice the lad. But as Abraham held the knife over his son, ready to kill him, there came to him the understanding that there were other and better ways of showing one's devotion to Jehovah than by taking human life, and that the ram he found in a near-by thicket was a more suitable sacrifice.

From this time onwards no son of Abraham might be offered as a sacrifice upon the altar, and though the Hebrews had yet much to learn, they had taken one step forward in their knowledge of what was the character of God and of what He required of them.

Soon after this Sarah died and Abraham mourned and wept for her. Her death made him realise, perhaps for the first time, that he had come a stranger into a strange land, for he had no family burying-place in which to bury her. He went to the people of the land, known as the Children of Heth or Hittites, and asked them if they would sell him the cave of Machpelah that he might use it as a burying-place. They would willingly have given it to Abraham as a gift, but he insisted on paying for it, probably in order that in days to come there might be no doubt as to the lawful possession of the land. In this cave he buried Sarah.

When Isaac had grown to be a man, in accordance with the custom of the East, Abraham chose a wife for him. He did not want one of the daughters of a Canaanite, for she would not have worshipped Jehovah, so he sent one of his most trusted servants to Mesopotamia to find a wife for his son amongst his own people. Laden with rich gifts, the servant went back to the old home of his master. There he met Rebekah, the granddaughter of his master's brother, who treated him with all the graciousness of eastern hospitality. He told his tale and Rebekah consented to return with him and become the bride of Isaac.

Not long afterwards Abraham, realising that he was growing old, gave all that he possessed to Isaac. Soon afterwards he died, full of years and beloved by all who served him. He was buried by the side of Sarah in the burial ground he had purchased.

JACOB

Isaac was mild and peace-loving, and his life lacked the adventure of that of his father; he and Rebekah lived the quiet, uneventful lives of rich herdsmen. They had two sons, Jacob and his older brother Esau. Esau was a hunter, living in the open air, and his father's favourite. Jacob, on the other hand, was his mother's favourite and he lived more in the tents than his brother. He must at this time have learnt all the details of a shepherd's life, for later on he was regarded as one well experienced in caring for flocks. It was perhaps because of the real help he was to Isaac and the responsibilities he carried, that he resented the fact that he was not the eldest son and would never have the eldest son's privileges. On one occasion when they were still young men Jacob, meeting Esau some way from home and finding him famished, took advantage of his condition, and tricked his brother into selling him his birthright for a mess of pottage. Esau does not seem to have regarded this seriously, but Jacob considered it a binding transaction.

As the years went by Isaac grew very rich. He had great flocks and herds and large numbers of servants who tended them. As he grew older, he became blind and very feeble, and when the time came that he realised that perhaps he might not live much longer, he desired to give his blessing to his oldest son. Amongst the ancient Hebrews, the blessing of the dying father was looked upon as a very solemn thing, and it gave the son who received it great importance in the eyes of the family. Isaac, knowing nothing of the bargain Jacob had made with his brother, sent for Esau and told him to go out and bring him in venison such as he loved. When he had eaten of it, he would give him his blessing. Rebekah, however, hearing this, persuaded Jacob into deceiving his father and taking the blessing given only to the oldest son. When Esau discovered what had happened, he declared he would kill Jacob, so Rebekah hastily sent him off to her brother Laban to wait until Esau's anger should have cooled.

Jacob started on his journey. When night fell, he found himself in a bleak and barren place, with no shelter, but he was strong and healthy and as a shepherd accustomed to nights in the open. So he took stones for his pillow and lay down to sleep. As he slept, he dreamed of a ladder reaching from earth to heaven, with angels going up and down it. Above the ladder stood Jehovah, who renewed to him the promise made to Abraham. Then Jacob awoke and a sense of awe came over him, and he set up a stone to mark the spot where God had seemed so near to him.

So Jacob and Esau separated for the time and Jacob went far away. Esau had been badly treated, but he lacked certain qualities that Jacob with all his faults possessed. Esau was a hunter, he loved the open air, but he had no great ambitions either for himself or for his family; he lived in the present and was content with the material satisfaction of his bodily needs. He was impulsive, but he had no imagination.

Jacob was just the opposite. He had many grave faults: he was selfish and jealous, he was willing to stoop to mean tricks to gain his ends, and he took by base deception the blessing of his father which was intended for Esau. But he had imagination, he could dream dreams and see visions. He had a passionate desire that the hopes of Abraham for his race should come true, and his faith in these hopes never left him.

Jacob continued his journey until he came to the place where his uncle Laban lived. He was welcomed and began at once to work for him. Laban had two daughters, Leah the older, Rachel the younger. And Jacob loved Rachel and bargained with Laban to serve him for seven years for no wages, if at the end of that time he would give him Rachel as his wife. Laban agreed and "Jacob served seven years for Rachel; and they seemed unto him but a few days, for the love he had to her."

When the seven years were over, Jacob asked Laban to give him Rachel for his wife as he had promised. Then Laban gathered together all the men of the place and made a feast. According to the eastern custom, on the marriage day a bride is veiled until the marriage ceremony is over, so Jacob did not see his bride's face until he had led her to his home. Then, when her veil was raised, behold, he had wedded Leah! And Jacob said to Laban: "What is this that thou hast done unto me? did I not serve with thee for Rachel? wherefore then hast thou beguiled me?" And Laban said: "It must not be so done in our country, to give the younger before the firstborn, but serve with me yet seven other years and thou shalt have Rachel also." Jacob did so, and at the end of another seven years Rachel became his wife and he loved her, we are told, more than he loved Leah.

After his marriage with Rachel, Jacob remained for some time longer with Laban. Eleven sons were born to him, and though still serving Laban, he began to grow rich himself in herds and flocks, he "increased exceedingly, and had much cattle, and maidservants, and menservants, and camels, and asses."

This growing prosperity of Jacob attracted the notice of the sons of Laban, who suspected him, and not unjustly, of having used trickery in getting some of this wealth. Jacob heard what they were saying of him, and noticing, too, that Laban was not as friendly to him as before, he decided to leave Haran and to return to his own land and the kindred whom he had left there long years before. So he started out with his wives and children, his servants and his flocks.

In spite of the years that had passed, Jacob was still afraid of the wrath of Esau, the brother whom he had so greatly wronged. So when he came near to the district where he knew Esau lived, he chose rich gifts from his flocks and sent them on in advance to his brother. Then when he and his family reached a brook that must be crossed, he sent his wives and children ahead, but he himself stayed behind alone.

It was night, and in the darkness there came to Jacob the greatest crisis he had yet had to face. Up to this moment, the outward story of his life had told one tale after another of selfishness, jealousy and deceit, of striving after material things, riches and possessions. But now in the loneliness and the darkness, he faced a struggle greater than any he had known before. In spite of all his wrong-doing, it was to Jacob that the promise once made to Abraham was renewed, and there must have been many an hour when he was watching his sheep that he had meditated deeply on the future of his race, when he had dreamed dreams and seen visions, and when the best that was in him had come uppermost. The story of what happened to him now, how alone in the darkness of the night he wrestled with an angel, was the ancient way of describing the struggle in the soul of Jacob which ended in the victory of his nobler and better self. He could not have triumphed had he never thought on things which were true and honest, just and pure. A man is, in a crisis, what his life beforehand has prepared him to be. The struggle of Jacob was not an easy struggle, and he did not come out of it unscathed, but he triumphed. From thenceforth Jacob was known by a new name. He was called Israel, which means a "prince," for as a prince he had struggled and been victorious.

The next morning Jacob met Esau and the brothers made their peace together. Then they went their separate ways again. Not long after, Jacob took his family to Bethel, the place where, when he was fleeing from the wrath of Esau, he had seen in a dream angels ascending and descending the ladder that reached to heaven. Bethel must always have been to him one of the holy places of his spirit, and once more he built an altar there to Jehovah. Then he journeyed on. When they were near Bethlehem, a son was born to Rachel, Benjamin, but Rachel died, and Jacob buried her there.

The Story of Joseph

Jacob now had twelve sons, of whom Joseph and Benjamin, the two youngest, were the sons of his favourite wife, Rachel. Because of this, and because they were the sons of his old age, he loved them more than the others, and Joseph in particular he spoiled. He dressed him in the long-sleeved tunic which was worn only by men who had no hard work to do, whilst his brothers were sent out to take care of the flocks.

Joseph seems to have thought of himself as superior to his brothers, for twice he told them of dreams that had come to him, which he interpreted as showing his father and his brothers bowing down in respect before him. All this made his brothers hate him, and the Hebrew story relates that one day when he had come out to see them in the fields, in their desire to be rid of him, they sold him as a slave to some merchants who happened to be passing on their way to Egypt.

On his arrival in Egypt, Joseph was sold to Potiphar, the captain of the Pharaoh's guard. He seems to have shown executive ability and common sense for he soon became the steward of Potiphar's household and one of his most trusted servants. Trusted as he was, however, Joseph was but a slave, and when an accusation was brought against him, though it was false, his master had no hesitation in sending him to prison. There he found as fellow-prisoners both the chief butler and the chief baker of the Pharaoh.

The people of the ancient world believed that important messages were often sent to them in dreams, and every one, from the highest to the lowest, paid great attention to them and sought their meaning. Whilst they were in the prison, both the butler and the baker had dreams. Disturbed as to what their meaning might be, they told them to Joseph. He interpreted them and his interpretation came true. This resulted in Joseph being brought to the notice of the Pharaoh. He, too, had strange dreams of which he sought the meaning. His wise men were unable to help him, but the chief butler, who had been restored to the favour of the Pharaoh, even as Joseph said would happen, told him of Joseph, the young Hebrew who was in prison and who possessed the gift of interpretation. Joseph was summoned to the presence of the Pharaoh, and was told of the dreams which he interpreted as a forecast of a serious famine in the land. As a reward for his interpretation he was made one of the great men of the kingdom. Through his ability and careful measures the grain supplies of Egypt were so safeguarded, that when the great famine came upon the land, the state storehouses were full and corn could be sold to the famished people.

This famine brought the brothers of Joseph to Egypt, for the famine extended to the land of Canaan, and they had heard that food was to be bought in Egypt. Joseph, having heard of their arrival, dramatically revealed himself as the brother whom they had so hated and despised. This made a great sensation in Egypt; the Pharaoh heard of it and invited the aged Jacob to come with his family to make his home there until the famine should be over. They came and were given the land of Goshen, where they lived with their flocks and herds until the death of Jacob. According to his wish, his sons took his body back to the land of Canaan. They buried him in the cave of Machpelah, where Abraham and Sarah, Isaac and Rebekah were buried, and where Jacob had buried Leah. They then returned to Egypt, which they seem to have regarded as their home.

As long as Joseph and the Pharaoh who had honoured him had been alive, all had gone well, but after their death the lot of the Hebrews became a very hard one. The Egyptians disliked foreigners and looked down on the occupation of shepherds, which they considered fit only for slaves; and so in time it came about that the Hebrews actually became the slaves of the Egyptians, who treated them very harshly. It was then that Moses appeared, who was to be their deliverer from Egypt.

CHAPTER V

MOSES AND THE EXODUS FROM EGYPT

THE Pharaoh who "knew not Joseph" was probably Ramses II, and he employed the Hebrews in work on his great buildings. The Hebrews had been increasing in numbers and Ramses seems to have been afraid that if they grew too numerous, there might be rioting. So he issued a decree that all their baby boys were to be killed.

One woman, however, saved her son by hiding him in a cradle by the river bank, where she hoped that no one would find him. But the Pharaoh's daughter coming down to the river with her maidens, found the little cradle with the Hebrew baby in it, and she took the child back with her to the palace and adopted him. She called him "Moses," a name which means "taken from the water." In this way it came about that Moses was brought up in the palace of the Pharaoh, where he learned all that an Egyptian prince would have been taught. He learned what the people of the East called the "wisdom of the Egyptians," which included some knowledge of astronomy, knowledge which was to be of great service to him later, and he learned how to command and rule people, a habit seldom or never learned by a slave, but which the man who was to lead the Hebrew people out of Egypt needed in a very great degree.

As he grew up, Moses used to visit the Hebrew

slaves and he was much interested in all that concerned them, but they distrusted him. They could hardly be expected to feel much confidence in a man who, though a Hebrew, lived in the palace of the Pharaoh who was oppressing them so cruelly. One day his sense of justice and anger was aroused at seeing one of the Egyptian overseers beating a Hebrew, and in impetuousness he killed the Egyptian. In the eyes of the law this was a great crime, and Moses was obliged to flee from the palace, as otherwise his life would have been in danger.

Up to this time Moses had been living as an Egyptian, but his act in killing the overseer put him definitely on the side of the Hebrew slaves. Now, out in the desert, whither he had fled, he was able to think quietly over the condition of his kinsmen, and there grew up in his mind the resolve to free them from their oppressors and to lead them back to the land which had been promised to their ancestor Abraham.

Moses spent some years in the desert as a shepherd, and these years gave him the training that was needed before he could become a great leader. He was near enough to Egypt to keep in touch with all that was taking place there. He learned to know the conditions of life in desert places, the discipline of his daily duty taught him that much in a great work depends on the steadfast perseverance in doing little things, and the quiet of the great spaces developed his powers of communion with Jehovah. At length the time came when he could enter upon the task to which he had dedicated his life.

One day, as Moses was tending his sheep, he saw in the distance a bush that was aflame with fire and yet it was not burnt up. As he drew near in order to see what was happening, he became conscious of a divine Presence and as he bowed himself in worship of Jehovah, there came to him the revealing conviction that the time had come for him to leave the quiet of the desert places and to return to Egypt to free his kinsmen from their bondage.

Accompanied by his brother Aaron, Moses returned to the city and entering the presence of the Pharaoh demanded the release of the Hebrews. It must have been a dramatic scene: the Pharaoh of Egypt on his throne, the symbol of the strength and glory of this world, confronted by Moses and Aaron, men from the desert, little more than slaves, but calm and serene in the strength of Jehovah.

The Pharaoh refused their petition, and the tasks given to the Hebrews were then increased and made so hard that it was almost impossible for them to be performed. When any Hebrew failed in what he was given to do, he was beaten.

The lot of the Hebrews was now so bitter, that some of them went to Moses and Aaron and blamed them for what had happened. Crushed and oppressed by their taskmasters, they could not see beyond the present and had neither the imagination nor the faith of Moses to believe that deliverance was possible.

Now Egypt was always subject to certain pestilences, and the country was evidently visited by some at this time. The Hebrew writer described them in great detail and attributed them all to the refusal of the Pharaoh to let the Hebrew slaves, who were very useful to him, leave the land. These calamities were known as the Ten Plagues. Not until after the last plague did the Pharaoh relent, but when in every Egyptian house of rich and poor alike, the firstborn lay dead, he sent for Moses and told him to begone, with his people and his flocks and his herds. Moses had been prepared for this. The angel of death had passed over the dwellings of the Hebrews, and while the Egyptians were bewailing their dead, the Hebrews were eating a meal. They ate it standing, staff in hand; their bundles with their belongings, together with gold and silver and warm garments given them by their Egyptian neighbours, tied up and ready to be shouldered. They ate the flesh of a lamb and unleavened bread, food that should strengthen them for the journey that lay ahead of them, a meal that should thenceforth be known to them as the Passover.

The Hebrews escaped. Coming down to the shore of the Red Sea they found that the east wind had blown with so much strength that the shallow waters of the sea were forced back, and they were able to cross in safety.

As soon as the Pharaoh heard that the Hebrews had really gone, he repented and pursued after them. But he arrived too late. He overtook them by the shore of the Red Sea, and as the Egyptians with their heavy chariots attempted to cross by the same passage as the Hebrews, the east wind changed, "the waters returned and covered the chariots, and the horsemen and all the host of Pharaoh that came into the sea after them, and the Egyptians were overthrown in the midst of the sea."

The Exodus was a tremendous moment in the history of the Hebrews. Behind them lay Egypt, with its fertile land, its broad river which served as a highway for the nations who traded with Egypt and added to its wealth, its busy cities, its learning —and slavery. Before them was the desert, silent, desolate, bare, apparently uninhabited, and—freedom. Behind them was the land where mind and spirit were bound by tradition, before them lay the silent places, but where was to be found freedom for mind and spirit.

The Hebrews were now able to continue their way secure against further attempts on the part of the Egyptians to pursue them. There were some thousands of them (we do not know the exact number), and they travelled as caravans still travel across the desert. A leader generally goes in front carrying a long pole on the top of which is a brazier filled with smoking coals. During the day the smoke can be seen at a great distance, so that the caravan can tell where the leader is and the direction in which it must travel. At night the glowing coals in the brazier serve the same purpose, and make it possible for travellers to take long night journeys over the desert in order to reach the oases without undue delay. Long years afterwards, when the history of this escape from Egypt was being written, it all seemed so miraculous to the Hebrew writer, that he described the journey over the trackless desert as guided by "the Lord who went before them, by day in a pillar of a cloud to lead them the way; and by night in a pillar of fire, to give them light; to go by day and night."

CHAPTER VI

THE MAKING OF THE HEBREW NATION

The Giving of the Law

SAFE from pursuit, the Hebrews journeyed first to Elim where they were refreshed by the wells of water and the palm trees. After leaving this cool and green oasis their road lay across a dreary strip of desert and here, it seemed as if their courage forsook them. They were hungry, and compared to their desert fare, the flesh pots they had left behind in Egypt seemed luxury. They grumbled and told Moses and Aaron they wished they had never started. Then it was that they were shown how to find manna, a bread-like food, that never failed them during their long desert wanderings.

It was about this time that the Hebrews met with their first real enemy. They were attacked by the Amalekites, a fierce people of that region. Joshua, whom we now hear of for the first time and who was later to make his mark as an able general, was sent out by Moses with a body of men to repulse the Amalekites: Moses did not fight, but he went up to the top of a hill from whence he could see the fighting, and there he lifted up his hands in prayer and supplication for his people. They were successful and repulsed the Amalekites and then went on their way with no further hindrance, but in their hearts they laid up vengeance on these people who had tried to stop them on their way to freedom.

The Hebrews now journeyed towards Sinai, a rocky peninsula, which is probably the only place in the world that has seen men come and go and yet itself remained unchanged since the beginning of history. It is a very awe-inspiring place, stern, bare, silent. A great encampment was made in the peninsula and the Hebrews stayed there for nearly a year.

Soon after their arrival at Sinai, Moses was joined by Jethro his father-in-law, who came with his wife and sons to the encampment. Up to this time, the relations between Moses and the people he led had been very simple. Every morning he sat in the door of his tent and received all who wanted to see him. He gave advice and settled quarrels and no one was ever turned away. Jethro observed this and realising that if it went on, the strength of Moses would be used up over a great many unnecessary details, he suggested that Moses should appoint elders whose business it should be to settle the less important questions, thus relieving him of an arduous work. This was done and proved to be the beginning of a more organised community.

The encampment of the Israelites had been made at the foot of Mount Sinai. Moses now gave instructions that bounds were to be set round the mountain beyond which the people were not to pass, for the mount was filled with the Presence of Jehovah and only Moses and his attendant might draw near. When this had been done, Moses went up to the top of the mountain where he spent forty days, communing with Jehovah and receiving inspiration for the writing of the Law.

The chief part of this Law is contained in what is known as the Ten Commandments. These laws taught the people two things: first, the duties they owed to Jehovah, and secondly, the duties they owed to each other. Many of the laws given by Moses to the Hebrews had reference only to the particular conditions of the time in which they lived, but the Ten Commandments have no such narrow interpretation, and they still serve as the foundation of the moral law of most civilised nations.

Up to this time the Hebrews had lived as disorganised tribes, but from now onwards, from the time when they had a law common to all alike, they had a growing feeling of kinship as sons of Israel, and they began to have a dim idea of what it meant to be a nation.

The Ten Commandments were written on two stone tablets, probably in much the same manner as that in which the Babylonians made their records. When Moses came down from the mountain, he found the people worshipping a golden calf which they had made in his absence. In his anger he threw down the tablets, and they were broken. Later, however, the Law was written out again and these second tables were kept in the Ark, a chest specially made for them. The idea of both the golden calf and of the Ark show the influence of Egypt on the Hebrews. Moses, like all great leaders, could see beyond the present, and he could disentangle and explain the difficulties of the moment by the light of the vision he had before him. When he saw the golden calf, he was right to be angry, for idolatry was one of the things that had to be stamped out. But the Hebrews, undisciplined and unable to look after themselves as they were, when they found themselves without their leader, in strange and unfamiliar surroundings, made an image of that which in Egypt had been held so sacred, the Bull that represented the Nile. Moses seemed to have deserted them, and in their ignorance of the true nature of Jehovah and their need for some visible leader they fell back upon the familiar Egyptian image. The Ark, too, was of Egyptian origin, for in Egypt, the Sun-God had his sacred boat in which he was taken by the priests on the days of the great processions. The Hebrew Ark was not made in the form of a ship, but of a chest, but the idea was the same, it was the means by which that which was sacred could be reverently carried about.

When an encampment was made anywhere, the Tabernacle or the Tent of Meeting was always set up a little outside the camp, in order that there might be a place of worship for the people. It was an oblong tent made of cloth and skins, divided into two parts: the Holy of Holies in which the Ark was kept and which might only be entered by the High Priest, and the Holy Place used for the daily services. These two parts were separated by a heavy veil or curtain. The court of the Tabernacle, where the people met, surrounded the tent, which was always set up, cared for, taken down and carried by the tribe of the Levites.

The Tabernacle was made in the wilderness from directions given to the people by Moses who had received the inspiration for the building of it from Jehovah. Freewill offerings were asked for and were made from the stores of things brought from Egypt: "Gold and silver and brass, and blue, and purple, and scarlet, and fine linen, and goats' hair, and rams' skins dyed red, and badgers' skins, and shittim wood, oil for the light, spices for anointing oil, and for sweet incense."

The Ark was made of shittim wood overlaid with gold, the lid of which was called the Mercy Seat. At the ends of the Mercy Seat were cherubim of gold with wings outstretched so that they met over the Ark. In the Holy Place was the altar of incense, the table of shewbread on which every sabbath day twelve cakes of bread made of fine flour were placed to be eaten by the priests, and the great golden candlestick. The altar of burnt offerings was in the court outside, and the whole was surrounded by curtains made of fine stuffs given by the people.

At length all was finished and everything set up in its place. Aaron, who was High Priest, and his sons who were priests, were robed in garments that had been specially made for them. In great reverence the people crowded to the Tabernacle, the Tent of Meeting, where, as Moses taught them, they might be more conscious of the Presence of Jehovah. And when the people were all assembled, Moses lifted up his hand and blessed them, saying:

The Lord bless you, and keep you:
  The Lord make his face shine upon you, and be
      gracious unto you:
  The Lord lift up his countenance upon you, and
      give you peace.[1]

From that day forth, whenever the Hebrews set out from an encampment the Ark preceded them, and as it was carried forward, Moses would lift up his hands and say:

Rise up, O Lord,
  And let thine enemies be scattered;
  And let them that hate thee flee before thee.

And when the next stopping-place had been reached and the Tabernacle set up and the Ark placed within the Holy of Holies, he would pray:

Return, O Lord,
  Unto the many thousands of Israel.[2]

Life in the Wilderness

Soon after leaving Mount Sinai, twelve men were sent into Canaan to spy out the land. They brought back a good account of its fertile valleys, but they also reported that the cities were strongly fortified and that the conquest of the land seemed an impossibility. The result of their report was that forty years went by before the Hebrews made any attempt to take possession of the country. The inhabitants of Canaan were highly civilised compared to the Hebrews, and there was much for the latter to learn before they could undertake such a task.

[1]Numbers vi, 24–26. [2]Numbers x, 35–36.

They were really only desert tribes; they called themselves the "Twelve Tribes of Israel," each bearing the name of one of the sons of Jacob. They knew nothing of attacking, far less of taking walled towns; the need for looking after their herds and flocks made sieges practically impossible for them, and their military knowledge was of a very elementary kind; they were only foot-soldiers, whereas the Canaanites had chariots of iron; so that a long period of training in the desert was necessary before they could become a fighting force to be reckoned with. Moses gave them this training during their long forty years' sojourn in the desert.

During these years the Hebrew people lived in the open air, exposed to all kinds of weather, and they were continually changing their place of encampment in the ceaseless search over the desert for springs of water. Their food was coarse and scanty, and the lack of water was a constant difficulty, making them long for the green hills and rich pasture lands flowing with milk and honey they hoped to find in Palestine. Besides the difficulty of not always finding enough to eat, there was added the danger that at any moment they might be attacked by the fierce nomad tribes of the desert.

The task of Moses was not an easy one. The people grumbled constantly, and once his authority was seriously threatened by a rebellion that broke out headed by three men, Korah, Dathan and Abiram. But in an earthquake which destroyed them and all they possessed the Hebrews saw the punishment of Jehovah, and they did not again seriously question the authority of Moses. Soon after this Aaron's authority was more firmly established, for amongst the twelve rods laid up in the Tabernacle as symbols of the twelve tribes of Israel, Aaron's was found to have budded with almond blossoms. This rod of Aaron was preserved in the Ark together with the portion of manna which had been set aside as a memorial of Jehovah's care for His people in their journeying through the wilderness.

The Hebrews now came into a desert region where they suffered greatly for want of water and they complained again that they had been brought from well-watered Egypt only to die in this thirsty land. Moses and Aaron withdrew into the Tabernacle where they prayed to Jehovah for guidance and wisdom in dealing with this unruly people. The word of Jehovah made known to Moses that if he struck a certain rock, he would find a spring and water would flow out. Then Moses, whose patience had been sorely tried by the people who owed him so much and repaid him with such querulous grumblings, struck the rock not once, but twice, saying, "Hear now, ye rebels, must we bring you water out of this rock?" The Hebrew writer, always bent on finding the moral meaning of events, tells us that because of this impatience, Jehovah refused to allow Moses to enter the Promised Land. Moses was old, and it was necessary that the leadership of the people should be entrusted to younger hands. The Hebrew historian, however, saw in Moses a life utterly devoted to Jehovah, and perhaps he seized upon this incident as the only comprehensible explanation of why the man, who had done such great things for his race, was forbidden the land of his desires.

On leaving this region, the Hebrews next came to Mount Hor, where Aaron died and was succeeded as High Priest by his son Eleazar.

The Hebrews then had to go down by the Red Sea in order to avoid the land of Edom, whose king had refused them passage through his land, even though they offered to pay for any supplies of food or water they needed. In this hot region a plague of poisonous serpents attacked them and large numbers of the people died. Then Moses had a brazen serpent made and set up where it could easily be seen, and we are told that whoever looked upon it was cured of the poison.

After the setting up of the brazen serpent not much is known of the halting places of the Hebrews until they reached the land of Moab and were approaching the River Jordan. Here again they asked permission of the kings of the district, Sihon, King of the Amorites and Og, King of Bashan, to let them pass through their lands unmolested. Again they were refused. This time they fought and the Israelites utterly defeated their enemies. These kings have become almost legendary, and their names stand as types of the fierce enemies Israel had to contend with and of signal victories they had gained before they could enter the Promised Land. Og, in particular, loomed very fiercely upon them; he was said to be a giant and his bedstead, made of iron, seems to have been kept as a curiosity on account of its great size.

The victories over these kings gave the Hebrews possession of a large stretch of country east of the Jordan. This so alarmed the inhabitants of the neighbouring lands, that they banded themselves together under Balak, King of Moab, and determined to fight the invaders. In order to obtain divine assistance Balak sent to Balaam, a wise man of that region, asking him to curse the people of Israel in order that they might be utterly destroyed. But instead of cursing them, Balaam blessed them and in words of great beauty foretold the coming of a day when a Star should rise out of Jacob and a Sceptre out of Israel and when dominion over the lands lying before them should be given to the people of Israel.

The discipline of the life in the desert gave the Hebrews the training they needed. They also grew accustomed to live together as an organised body of people, until at last the time came when they were ready to enter the land of Canaan with every likelihood of being victorious. But Moses did not live to go with his people into the Promised Land. He knew that he was old and that he must give up the leadership to one better equipped than he for the hard fighting that he knew would be necessary before they could settle in Canaan. He sent for Joshua, who had already shown ability as a military leader and was trusted by the people, and in the sight of all Israel he handed over his authority to him: "Be strong and of a good courage," he said to him, "for thou must go with this people unto the land which the Lord hath sworn unto their fathers to give them; and thou shalt cause them to inherit it. And the Lord, he it is that doth go before thee; he will be with thee, he will not fail thee, neither forsake thee; fear not, neither be dismayed."[1]

Tradition says that Moses went up the mountain of Nebo to the top of Pisgah whence he had a view of the Promised Land, and that he died there, but no one has ever known where his grave was. An old legend still survives among the modern Arab inhabitants of this region, that a certain moaning of the wind heard there from time to time is the sighing of Moses in sorrow that he must leave his people and the mountains he loved so well.

The death of Moses marks the end of the first period of the history of the Hebrews, for after they had entered and conquered Canaan, they were no more a nomad, shepherd people. As the Hebrews looked back to Abraham as the founder of their nation, so did they look back to Moses as their Lawgiver. It is true that he laid the foundations of Hebrew law and in the Ten Commandments the foundations of a much wider law, but Moses was more than a lawgiver, he was a great religious teacher and a leader of men. Under circumstances of extraordinary difficulty he converted an undisciplined horde of discontented slaves into a community that had at least the beginnings of the idea of law and order and into men who could fight and win battles. Humble-minded, loyal to Jehovah and

[1]Deuteronomy xxxi, 7–8.

his race, and of undismayed courage, he accomplished what a lesser man would never even have dreamed of undertaking. The Hebrew writer of the book of Numbers described Moses as "very meek, above all the men which were upon the face of the earth." The meekness which characterised Moses was that which may perhaps best be described as a disciplined surrender of the will to God. In every action, in all his teaching, Moses was guided not by his own desires but by what he, to the best of his powers, believed to be the will of Jehovah. "And there arose not a prophet since in Israel like unto Moses, whom the Lord knew face to face."

CHAPTER VII

THE CONQUEST OF CANAAN AND THE AGE OF THE JUDGES

The Taking of the Land

UNDER Joshua the Israelites prepared to cross the Jordan and enter the Promised Land. Before advancing, Joshua determined to find out all he could as to the strength of Jericho, the first city to be taken. He sent two men to spy secretly, telling them to find out all they could as to the strength of the city and how best it could be attacked. They set out, and on reaching Jericho were given a lodging in the house of a woman named Rahab. But it was told the King of Jericho that Hebrew spies had come into the city and he sent out men to search for them. Rahab seems to have been friendly towards them for, on hearing that the house was to be searched, she took them up to the flat roof and hid them under the flax which was spread out there in the sun. When the king's men came, she told them that she had seen the men for whom they were searching, but that they had gone away and she did not know where. As a reward for having hidden them, Rahab asked the spies to save her and her household when they took Jericho. They promised to do so, if she would put a red cord in her window so that the house might be recognised. She did as they asked and they kept their word.

The spies returned to Joshua with their report and all was made ready to cross the Jordan. At certain periods landslides occur in the valley of the Jordan, causing part of the river to be dammed up. Joshua had chosen such a time for the Israelites to cross, as it enabled them to go over comparatively easily. It must have been a solemn and a thrilling moment as the long procession crossed and each man's foot touched the Land of Promise, the goal of their long wandering. As a memorial Joshua commanded that twelve stones, one for each of the twelve tribes, should be set up in the place where they had crossed. It was done, and they stood there for long ages as an outward symbol of the thankfulness of Israel to Jehovah.

The Israelites now advanced to the city of Jericho which they besieged. It was not a long siege and the inhabitants soon surrendered to the strange people from the desert, who marched round their walls, blowing fiercely on their trumpets. To later generations the taking of Jericho seemed miraculous, and the tale was told of how the walls themselves fell down to admit the people of Jehovah.

A primitive Semitic custom required that on occasions when a city was captured, all the inhabitants and their property should be *devoted* to the god of the conqueror, a custom that meant the complete destruction of everything belonging to the conquered people. Joshua followed this custom and gave strict orders that when Jericho was taken, no one should keep any prisoner or any of the plunder for himself. Everything was to be *devoted* to Jehovah. In spite, however, of Joshua's command, one man took some silver and gold and rich Babylonian garments and hid them in his tent. Meanwhile the Israelites had gone from Jericho to the city of Ai. But instead of the victory which they expected, they were badly defeated. The task of conquering Canaan was a very hard one, and Joshua knew that it could only be accomplished by maintaining absolute discipline amongst his fighting men. He was sure that if for one moment discipline were relaxed and the men began to think of their own personal greed for plunder and booty, they would be unable to hold their own against the Canaanites. So he held a thorough investigation. It was found that a man named Achan had kept some of the plunder for himself and convinced that only by making a terrible example of the results of disobedience would he prevent a constant recurrence of it, Joshua decreed that Achan and his family should be stoned to death, and that all his possessions should be burnt with fire. To us, it seems reasonable that Achan should be punished, though the actual punishment seems an unduly harsh one, but it is difficult to see why his family and his property should have shared his fate. But the times were merciless, and to Joshua this seemed the only way of compelling the military obedience that was necessary to carry out the work in hand.

Joshua now once more attacked Ai and was victorious. As a result the greater part of the south of Canaan fell into his hands. This very much alarmed the neighbouring kings, and they made a league together against Israel. But the men of Gibeon, hearing what Joshua had done to Jericho and Ai, thought it a better policy to make a league with Israel, and they attempted to do so by craft. Pretending that they had come from a far country, they put on old and dusty garments, put mouldy bread in their bundles and went to Joshua. When he asked them who they were and from whence they came, they answered: "From a very far country thy servants are come because of the name of the Lord thy God: for we have heard the fame of him and all that he did in Egypt."

They had actually come to terms with Joshua and the elders of Israel before it was discovered that instead of coming from a far distance, they lived near at hand on the very borders of their land, and controlled a pass that would be of great value to the Israelites. They could not be destroyed, as the people in their anger at having been deceived would have liked, because of the peace made with them. Instead of treating them as equals, however, Joshua declared that the Gibeonites should thenceforth be as slaves to Israel, and should be to them their hewers of wood and drawers of water.

Joshua then passed on through the land of Canaan. He conquered not only the south, but the centre, and then the north. When he had subdued the whole land, he divided it amongst the twelve tribes, giving to each a definite portion of land.

This conquest had taken some time and it was not a peaceful one, but as at Jericho, it was accompanied by fearful massacres of the Canaanites and often the complete destruction of their cities. The Hebrews looked upon these wars as religious wars, they were not only taking possession of the land promised to them, but they were showing to the world that in that land they would tolerate no belief in any God but Jehovah. Later Hebrew writers regretted the cruelty with which these wars were accompanied, but the standards of those early days demanded that evil should be conquered by violence, and the people believed that Jehovah was pleased that His enemies should be completely exterminated.

When the land had been divided amongst the twelve tribes, the Tabernacle was permanently set up at Shiloh, and then a great assembly of the people took place at Shechem. Joshua was now an old man, and he made a last speech to the people. He reminded them of all that Jehovah had done for them and entreated them never to forsake Him, no matter what temptations might come from the heathen people round about them. And the people promised him solemnly that they would do as he bade them. "The Lord our God will we serve," they promised, "and His voice will we obey."

Customs in Early Israel

The conquest and settlement of Canaan was the first great change in the history of the Hebrew people, for from being shepherd tribes, living in their tents and wandering from place to place in search of food and water for themselves and their flocks, they became a settled people with fixed homes. They changed from a nomadic life to an agricultural one, they became husbandmen as well as herdsmen.

The conquest meant also the impact of a new civilisation on a people that for forty years had been living the life of Bedouins in the desert. They never completely drove out the Canaanites, from whom they learnt many things. Town life developed and the old simplicity began gradually to disappear. The conquest of the land meant that they now possessed "cities which they had not built, and houses full of all good things which they had not filled, and wells digged which they had not digged, vineyards and olive trees which they had not planted."

This settled way of living very soon developed in the Hebrew a strong feeling towards his own property, and it became his ideal to possess his own vineyard and field. Houses were built, and village settlements grew up, but there was no unity of government, every man did that which was right in his own eyes. Nevertheless the Law by which the Hebrew lived emphasised the fact that he was living in a community and had therefore duties and obligations towards others who lived there with him. Much of the early Hebrew law was similar to that of Babylon. It was that of an "eye for an eye and a tooth for a tooth," a harsh code, but a step in advance of the unlimited revenge which had been the earlier system. The Hebrew law had also another side to it, one that was civilising and humane, and there were ideals enshrined in it that gave promise of greater moral progress in the future.

The stranger, the orphan and the widow were to be protected: "Thou shalt neither vex a stranger, nor oppress him: for ye were strangers in the land of Egypt. Ye shall not afflict any widow, or fatherless child. If thou afflict them in any wise, and they cry at all unto me, I will surely hear their cry."[1]

Kindness was to be shown to a personal enemy: "If thou meet thine enemy's ox or his ass going astray, thou shalt surely bring it back to him again. If thou see the ass of him that hateth thee lying under his burden, and wouldest forbear to help him, thou shalt surely help with him."[2]

A slave was to be set free after six years of service, unless he chose to remain with his master: "If thou buy an Hebrew servant, six years he shall serve: and in the seventh he shall go out free for nothing. If he came in by himself, he shall go out by himself: if he were married, then his wife shall go out with him. If his master have given him a wife, and she have borne him sons or daughters; the wife and her children shall be her master's, and he shall go out by himself. And if the servant shall plainly say, I love my master, my wife and my children; I will not go out free: then his master shall bring him unto the judges; he shall also bring him to the door, or unto the door post; and his master shall bore his ear through with an awl; and he shall serve him for ever."[3]

An injured slave was to be set free. "If a man smite the eye of his servant, or the eye of his maid, that it perish; he shall let him go free for his eye's

[1]Exodus xxii, 21–23. [2]Exodus xxiii, 4–5. [3]Exodus xxi, 2–6.

sake. And if he smite out his manservant's tooth, or his maidservant's tooth; he shall let him go free for his tooth's sake."[1]

All through the Law, in spite of a background of crude hardness, there is this emphasis on kindly dealings and humane conduct, especially towards the stranger, for the Hebrew knew out of his own experience what it was to be oppressed and a stranger in the land in which he dwelt. "Thou shalt not oppress a stranger: for ye know the heart of a stranger, seeing ye were strangers in the land of Egypt."[2]

Judges in Israel

The Israelites were now settled in Canaan, but they were still groups of separate tribes rather than a nation, and they had no king. Jehovah the Lord of Hosts was their king. The Canaanites who were still in the land and on their borders made constant war on them, and when these crises arose, local leaders called Judges appeared who took command and by their courage and daring delivered the people from their foes.

This period of the Judges probably lasted a little over three hundred years. The story is told in the book of Judges, a collection of old tales and traditions, many of them very primitive, tales that show the faith of Israel as not always very firm, for exposed to the pagan influences surrounding them, the Hebrews often fell into paganism themselves. But underneath these tales of heroes and doughty

[1]Exodus xxi, 26–27. [2]Exodus xxiii, 9.

champions, rough and crude as they are, is the pervading faith of the writer that Jehovah was at all times the King and Head of Israel, and that faith in Him brought victory and denial of Him defeat and trouble.

One of the fiercest of the wars during this period was waged against the King of Canaan, the captain of whose host was Sisera. Israel was judged at this time by a woman, Deborah, who gave good and wise counsel to those who sought her aid. She sent for a man called Barak and commissioned him to go at the head of an army and fight against Sisera who was invading the land. He went and won a great victory, but Sisera himself escaped and fled to the tent of a friend. The man was away, but Jael, his wife, came out to meet Sisera and she begged him to enter the tent and to have no fear. He asked for a drink of water and she offered him milk in her best dish, she brought him butter, probably the curds eaten in the desert, she led him to the couch in the tent and covered him with a cloak, bidding him rest and sleep without fear of his enemies. Then, as he lay asleep, she slew him. When Barak came in hot pursuit, she led him into the tent saying: "Come, and I will show thee the man whom thou seekest." And there lay Sisera dead.

There was great rejoicing at the victory, and Deborah and Barak gave voice to the feelings of the people in a song of praise. This song is one of the oldest parts of the Bible and is full of great and dramatic poetry. It is a very fierce song in places, but it must be judged by the standards of the time and not by those which a fuller knowledge of the character of God has given to a later age. The Hebrews of the days of the Judges still believed that Jehovah desired the destruction of those who did not believe in Him and who were the enemies of His chosen people. In the eyes of Deborah and Barak the deed of Jael was not an act of treachery, but a righteous vengeance descending upon an enemy of Jehovah. It must be remembered, too, that the Hebrews were no fiercer or more cruel in war than were the nations surrounding them, and not as cruel as some. They must be judged by what they knew and not by what we know, and whatever they may not have known, one thing their leaders did know and believe with an unfaltering faith was that Jehovah, the God of Righteousness, would ultimately triumph over all evil.

The next enemy that rose up against Israel was Midian. Because the Canaanites had never been entirely driven out of the land, the Israelites were constantly tempted to forsake Jehovah and to worship the false gods of their neighbours. This had happened now, and an altar had been set up to Baal in the place where Gideon, a strong and able warrior, dwelt. Determined to deliver his land from her foes, he began by destroying the altar of Baal. He dared not do it by day, so one night he took ten of his servants and broke down the altar. "And when the men of the city arose early in the morning, behold, the altar of Baal was cast down. And they said one to another, Who hath done this thing? And when they inquired and asked, they were told,

Gideon, the son of Joash, hath done this thing. Then the men of the city said unto Joash, Bring out thy son, that he may die: because he hath cast down the altar of Baal." Gideon was spared, but this had brought him into the notice of the people. The story tells us that the Midianites and the Amalekites, and the children of the East gathered together, and pitched in the valley of Jezreel in order to fight Israel. Then the Spirit of the Lord came upon Gideon. He blew a trumpet, the people gathered after him, and they all prepared for battle. By a series of tests, Gideon then reduced his army to a comparatively small number of men who knew how to fight, who would be quick and able in an emergency and on whose loyalty he could rely. With this army he defeated the Midianites and drove them out of the land.

The Israelites were not to possess their land in peace for long, however, for next the Ammonites made war against them. This time the people made Jephthah the Gileadite, a mighty man of valour, head and captain over them. Before going out to battle Jephthah, simple, rugged and superstitious, made a vow to Jehovah, that if victory were granted to him, whatever first came out from his house to meet him on his return should be offered as a sacrifice to Jehovah. He fought the Ammonites and defeated them, we are told, with a great slaughter. Then he returned in triumph to his home. As he came to his house, his daughter, his only child, a fair and lovely maiden, came out to meet him, singing and dancing with joy. But when her father told her of his vow, in her tender love for him and thinking only of his sorrow and not of her pain, she accepted her fate without a question. Her father had won a great victory and Israel was saved; if she were the price of the victory, then she would pay it gladly. In the midst of tales of rough and bloodthirsty courage, the story of Jephthah's daughter, we are not told her name, stands out as one of delicate grace and tenderness.

Samson, the Strong Man

Again enemies beset the Israelites, and this time it was the Philistines who lived on their western borders. They had always been their enemies, and they were always to give them trouble. The Philistines were a strong people, fierce fighters, but not wholly uncivilised. They had five strong towns and important trade routes passed through their land.

Living near the Philistine border was a young man of the tribe of Dan whose name was Samson. He was a Nazirite, one of those who were bound by a special vow to keep alive the old primitive ideals of the Bedouin. The Nazirite was not allowed to drink wine or any other strong drink, neither was he allowed to have his hair shorn. It had been prophesied of Samson that he would deliver Israel from the Philistines, and we are told that he was possessed of the most extraordinary strength. The story goes on to tell us how he loved a woman whose name was Delilah and took her for his wife.

The Philistines were still attacking Israel, but

the great strength of Samson prevented them from gaining any permanent successes. Then it was that the lords of the Philistines went to Delilah and promised to give her money if she would find out from Samson wherein lay his great strength. She yielded to the temptation and begged him to tell her the secret. At first he put her off with false answers, but at length he told her that his strength lay in his hair which had never been shorn. Then Delilah, when he was asleep, cut off his hair. When he woke his strength was gone, and she delivered him to his enemies. The Philistines took him to Gaza, where they tortured him and put out his eyes, and then they threw him into prison.

Samson does not seem to have used his strength as he might have done for the real and lasting deliverance of Israel from the Philistines. He was always engaged in quarrels with them, but they were generally personal quarrels, and time after time he committed deeds of violence against them in order to be avenged of some personal insult. Tradition has handed down strange tales of the deeds he performed: how he killed a lion with the ease with which most men would have slain a kid, how he slew a thousand men with the jawbone of an ass, and how on the day of his death he destroyed with his hands the great hall in which the lords of the Philistines were feasting. Samson seems to belong to a rougher, more primitive time even than the earlier Judges, and it is probable that the tales of his exploits belong to the folklore of the time rather than to its real history.

The Story of Ruth

In great contrast to the rough story of Samson is the idyllic tale of Ruth. Once during the period of the Judges there was a serious famine in the land, and a certain man who lived in Bethlehem went with Naomi his wife and his two sons to the land of Moab, where they lived for some years. The two sons married Moabite maidens, Orpah and Ruth, but soon after both the sons and their father died, leaving Naomi alone with her daughters-in-law. Feeling lonely in a strange country, and knowing that the famine in her own land was over, Naomi determined to return home, but her daughters-in-law were young and she thought life would be happier for them if they remained with their own people. Orpah consented, and went back to her father's house, but Ruth refused. "Intreat me not to leave thee," she said to Naomi, "or to return from following after thee: for whither thou goest, I will go; and where thou lodgest, I will lodge; thy people shall be my people, and thy God my God: where thou diest, will I die, and there will I be buried: the Lord do so to me, and more also, if aught but death part thee and me!"

Naomi and Ruth returned to Bethlehem, where Ruth went out to glean in the fields of Boaz, a kinsman of Naomi. It was the Hebrew custom that when the harvest had been gathered in, the ears of corn that had not been put into the sheaves should be left lying in the field for any one who needed them. Ruth, a stranger in the place, was noticed by

Boaz. He made inquiries about her, and on learning who she was, and of her love and loyalty to Naomi, he bade her glean only in his field, and he gave instructions to his young men that they should leave plenty of grain lying where she could gather it. All through the days of the harvesting and gleaning Boaz treated Ruth with gentle courtesy. When work stopped for a midday rest and food, he not only saw that she had food, but waited on her himself.

According to Jewish custom, because of his kinship with Naomi it was the duty of Boaz to find a husband for Ruth. But he loved her himself and Ruth became his wife. And she bore him a son whose name was Obed, and Obed was the father of Jesse, and Jesse was the father of David.

Samuel, the Last Judge

There was a certain man whose name was Elkanah, and his wife was called Hannah. Every year Elkanah went to Shiloh to worship and Hannah went with him. But there was great sorrow in her heart, for she had no child. On one occasion when she was in Shiloh, she offered up her prayer to Jehovah, weeping and vowing that if Jehovah would grant her prayer and give her a son, she would dedicate him to the service of the Lord all the days of his life.

Eli, the aged High Priest, was sitting not far from Hannah and he noticed her, and when he found out that she was very earnestly offering some petition to God, he said to her: "Go in peace and may the God of Israel grant thee thy petition that thou hast asked of him." And Hannah's petition was granted. She had a son, and she called him Samuel, a name which means "asked of the Lord."

When the child was old enough to leave home, his mother brought him to Shiloh and left him there with Eli to serve him in the Tabernacle. And every year Hannah made him a little coat which she brought up with her when she came with her husband to offer the yearly sacrifice.

Samuel waited on Eli, and as Eli began to grow blind it was the child who tended the lamps in the Tabernacle and who took care of the sacred vessels used in the sanctuary. He was full of gentle courtesy, and not only Eli, but all who came to worship at Shiloh loved him.

Eli was very old. He had two sons, who were priests. They were wicked and people hated them and began to talk about their wrongdoing, but Eli, though he pleaded with them to leave off their evil ways, was unable to control them.

One night Samuel, who slept not far from Eli, suddenly awoke, conscious that he had heard a voice calling him. He thought it was Eli who needed something and he ran in to him and asked what he wanted. But Eli had not called and sent the child back to bed. Again Samuel heard the voice, and again Eli bade him lie down, for he had not called and needed nothing. A third time in the quiet and the stillness of the night, Samuel heard the voice calling him, and again he went to Eli. This time the old man knew that it was God who was speaking to the spirit of Samuel and he told him that if he heard the voice again, he was to say: "Speak, Lord, for thy servant heareth!"

Samuel did as he was told and lay down again. Then in the silence God spoke to him and gave him a message for Eli concerning the dreadful fate that awaited his sons.

As Samuel grew older, his influence began to grow. Eli was so old and blind, that the people looked to the younger man who had grown up in his service for help and guidance. They recognised the simple piety of his nature and regarded him as a prophet sent to them from God.

At this time Israel was again at war with the Philistines. Things were going badly with Israel, and the leaders of the army sent to Shiloh and demanded that the Ark be sent to them so that the symbol of the Presence of Jehovah might bring them victory. But it was in vain; the Israelites were repulsed with great loss, the two sons of Eli were among the slain, and most serious of all, the Ark was taken by the enemy. The evil tidings were brought back to Shiloh by a man who had escaped, and when Eli heard that the Ark was in the hands of the heathen unbelievers in Jehovah, he fell off the seat on which he was sitting and broke his neck and died.

The Philistines had taken the Ark to Ashdod, and they set it up in the temple of their god Dagon. But all kinds of misfortunes fell upon the Philistines: the image of Dagon fell down mysteriously and then a pestilence broke out. These things were attributed to the presence of the God of Israel, and so the Ark was moved first to Gath and then to other places. But wherever the Ark was taken, there the pestilence at once appeared. This lasted for seven months, and then the Philistines determined to return the Ark to Israel. Their wise men told them to place the Ark on a new cart, together with jewels as a peace-offering to the God of Israel. They were to harness oxen which had never yet borne a yoke to the cart, and then, if the oxen went of their own accord to the land of Israel, they might know that it was Jehovah who had brought the pestilence upon the Philistines, but if the oxen did not turn towards Israel, then it was not the hand of Jehovah that had smitten them, but a chance that had happened to them.

Everything was done as the wise men ordered, and five lords of the Philistines accompanied the Ark to see what would happen. The cattle started and turned their heads straight towards the land of Israel. This was enough for the Philistine lords and they returned home. The cattle went on until they reached Bethshemesh, where the men of the place were gathering in the harvest. When they saw the Ark approaching, they went to meet it with great joy and offered a thanksgiving to Jehovah for its recovery. Then the Ark was taken to Kirjath-jearim, where it remained for some years in the house of Abinadab, whose son was set apart to care for it.

Samuel now lived in Ramah and for many years he was the Judge in Israel, going from Ramah to

Bethel and Gilgal and other places and then returning to his home. The Israelites had now had Judges for nearly three hundred years, but no king. Under pressure, however, from constant attacks from the Philistines, they began to realise that in order to preserve their much threatened independence, they should be united at all times under one leader, and so they demanded a king, like the nations that surrounded them. They naturally turned for advice to Samuel, and they were obliged to tell him, that much as they revered and honoured him, his sons whom he had made Judges in different parts of the land were not following in his footsteps. After his death the people would have no one whom they respected and trusted to deliver them from their foes.

Samuel did not meet their request with much sympathy. At first he tried to dissuade them from changing their old tribal form of government, a change which he feared would shake their loyalty to Jehovah, and he drew for them a very vivid picture of the autocracy of the oriental king. He finally agreed, however, to find a man who should have the qualities necessary to make a good king, and his choice fell upon one called Saul. Samuel anointed him with oil (according to the old traditions in the East, anointing with oil always meant being set apart for some definite task), and then he presented him to the people as their king. And when the people saw Saul, they all shouted and cried: "God save the King!"

And so Saul became the first king of Israel.

CHAPTER VIII

THE UNITED KINGDOM OF ISRAEL

Saul, the Warrior

SAUL began his reign well. Israel was surrounded by enemies who were attacking her and Saul, who proved to be a good general, led out the army and conquered them. He defeated both the Ammonites and the Philistines and then he attacked the Amalekites.

It will be remembered that soon after the Israelites had crossed the Red Sea, they had been attacked by the Amalekites, a fierce tribe, who had wanted to prevent them passing by the land where they dwelt. The Amalekites had been defeated, but the Israelites had never forgotten how they had made an unprovoked attack upon them, and Saul determined to be avenged. Samuel so fully believed that enemies of Israel were also enemies of Jehovah and that Jehovah would be glad to see them all exterminated, that he actually thought the idea which came to him of warring against the Amalekites until they were utterly destroyed came from Jehovah. But when the war was over Saul, instead of following the instructions given him by Samuel, spared Agag, the king of the Amalekites, and the best of the sheep and the oxen on the pretext that he would offer them later in sacrifice to Jehovah.

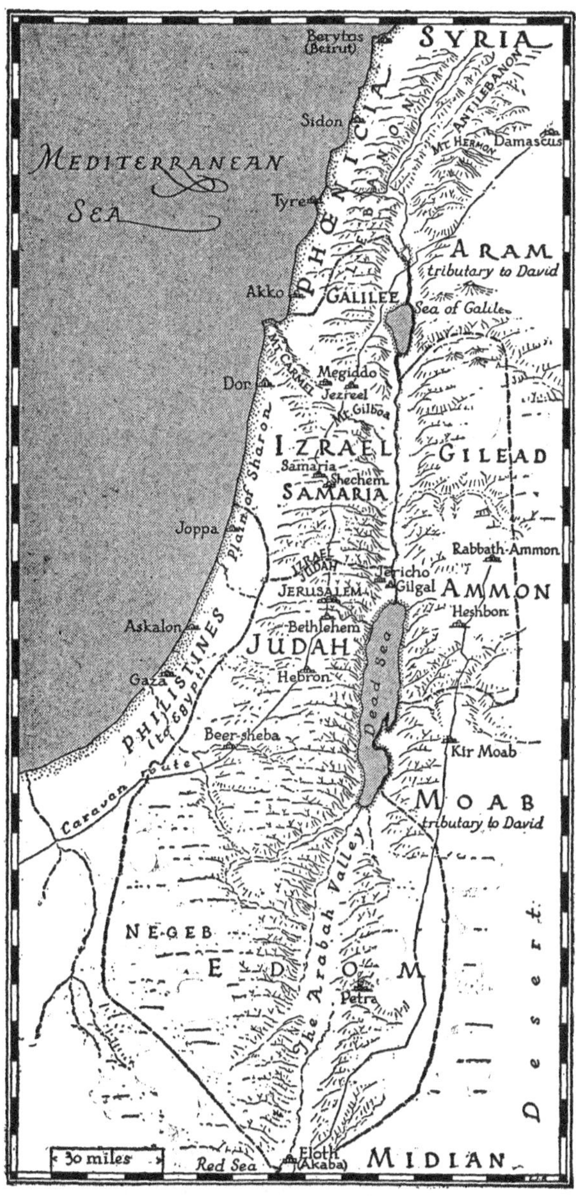

The United Kingdom of Israel

But Samuel would not accept this excuse and Agag was mercilessly put to death.

The scene between Samuel and Saul marks a turning point in Saul's career. The king had been convicted by the aged Judge of the sin of disobedience, a very grave sin in the eyes of the early Hebrews. All through their history, written not as a mere narrative of events that had taken place, but as the history of the Hebrew people in their relation to Jehovah, there is constant emphasis on the necessity of obedience to the will of God. The fact that in the early days of their history they were mistaken in what they thought was the character of God does not take away from the moral splendour of the uncompromising belief of their teachers that righteousness consisted in obedience, in the surrender of the human will to that of God.

Samuel was an old man, old-fashioned and prejudiced. Had he possessed the capacity of sharing the visions of the young, he might have understood Saul better and given to him something of his own staunchness of character. But at this turning point in the history of Israel, when as a united kingdom she was about to take her place in the ancient world, Samuel stands as a rugged figure, calling upon king and people to take heed to the commandments of God.

Saul had proved himself a good general, and he had strengthened Israel against her enemies, but he had shown himself to be both impatient and impetuous, and in other ways that were more marked later, to be weak and lacking in strength of character to carry out all that he knew to be right. Samuel knew this and he began to doubt whether Saul's family were the right one to reign over Israel. He finally came to the conclusion that the next king must be sought for elsewhere. Guided by the spirit of Jehovah he went to Bethlehem, where, out of the eight sons of a man named Jesse, he chose the youngest, David, a shepherd lad, and in the presence of his brothers he anointed him as the future king of Israel.

Saul and David

Just at this time Saul became ill. He was said to be tormented by an evil spirit, the ancient way of describing any disease of the mind. This disease would attack the king suddenly; at times it would plunge him into gloomy melancholy and at others it would excite his mind with unreasonable and malicious rage. It was thought that perhaps music would soothe him, and David the young shepherd at Bethlehem, known as a skilful harpist and sweet singer, was sent for. He came to Saul and his music restored the king to health, and Saul loved him and made him one of his armour-bearers.

David quickly became very popular. Young, good-looking, strong and a brave soldier, he also had great skill both as a musician and poet, and his winning manner made him friends everywhere. But Saul's affection for him soon turned to jealousy. The Israelites were again at war with the Philistines, and during this war David slew the giant

Goliath, who had challenged the Israelite army to send out a champion to fight him. The people welcomed back the young hero with enthusiasm, and gave him even greater praise than they had ever given Saul himself.

> Saul hath slain his thousands,
> And David his ten thousands,

was their welcoming song, and Saul's mind, still weak from his illness, became so overclouded with jealousy that his madness returned. His old affection for David turned to hate and he tried to kill him several times. It is probable that Saul knew David had been anointed by Samuel to take his place as king, and that this added to his hate and jealousy. David, however, never attempted to take the throne during Saul's lifetime, neither did he ever give the king grounds for fearing that he would make such an attempt.

Saul had a son Jonathan, a gallant youth, chivalrous and loyal to those whom he loved. He and David became close friends, and when Jonathan found out that his father wanted to kill David, he arranged for his friend's escape.

David first took refuge at Nob where the priest of the place gave him food and the sword of Goliath, which had been kept there amongst his treasures. From there David went to the Cave of Adullam, where his brothers and a great many of his friends and followers joined him. It was a motley band. There were young men, hero-worshippers of David, who were indignant at the way Saul had treated him; there were the discontented, the unemployed, men who were in debt, men who were homeless. There were about four hundred men in all and David became a captain over them.

Saul was so afraid that the popularity of David might make the people proclaim him king, that he pursued him in the hope that he might capture him and take his life. He soon discovered that David had taken refuge in the Cave of Adullam, and then news was brought to him of the help that had been rendered David by the priest at Nob. In order to show what might be expected by any one who attempted to give shelter or assistance of any kind to the fugitive, Saul gave orders that the priest and all that belonged to him were to be destroyed. Saul's own servants refused to kill a priest of Jehovah, so the man who brought the tale to Saul, an Edomite, was sent to carry out the brutal order.

Thus did Saul avenge himself on those who had helped one who had never given him anything but loyalty and affection. The times were rough and cruel and men did not often show any mercy to their enemies, but David was no enemy to the king. David himself could be cruel, but he understood, as few men of his time understood, what it was to be loyal in friendship.

A messenger now came to Saul summoning him to return for the Philistines were again invading the land. During this war with the Philistines, David, in the Cave of Adullam, found himself cut off from some of his usual supplies. He wanted water, but the Philistines had made Bethlehem their headquarters and the wells were in their hands. A great longing for water from the wells of his home came over David and he said: "Oh, that one would give me drink of the water of the well of Bethlehem, that is at the gate!" Three of his friends took him at his word, broke through the Philistines' line, drew water from the well, and brought it back to him in triumph. But David refused to drink it, and he poured it out. "My God forbid it me," he said, "that I should do this thing: shall I drink the blood of these men that have put their lives in jeopardy; for with the jeopardy of their lives they brought it." It was not surprising that such a man had loyal and devoted followers.

In spite of all Saul's unkindness to him, David still loved him. Twice he had Saul in his power and might have killed him, as any other man of his time undoubtedly would have done and without receiving any blame, but David spared him.

Samuel died about this time, and though Saul had not seen him for a long time, the thought of the aged Judge must sometimes have exercised a restraining influence on the king. But now all restraint was gone; Samuel was dead, the Philistines were growing stronger and were again invading the land, and when Saul turned to Jehovah to ask Him to give some sign as to what he should do in this time of danger, there was no answer. Now for some time there had been men in Israel, wizards, who had professed to be able to speak with those who had died, and in some cases even to call back their spirits to speak with those who desired to communicate with them. Believing that this was a wrong practice and that it could give rise to all kinds of cheating and deception, Saul had commanded that all such wizards should leave the land. But now, feeling that through his own fault he was forsaken by Jehovah, realising probably that through his jealousy and weakness of character he had failed to live up to the good beginnings of his reign, and yet still proud and unwilling to admit his wrongdoing, he was conscience-stricken and frightened. In his despair he turned to the very practice that he had condemned and forbidden in others. He went to the witch who lived at Endor and asked her to bring the spirit of Samuel before him. She did as he asked, but Samuel had for him only words of grave warning of the doom that was shortly to fall on him.

In dismay Saul went back to his army to march against the Philistines. It was his last battle. Israel was defeated and Saul and Jonathan slain. The news was brought to David by a man who had escaped from the battle and when he heard it David sorrowed greatly and lamented for them, saying:

The beauty of Israel
Is slain upon thy high places!
How are the mighty—
Fallen!

Tell it not in Gath,
Publish it not in the streets of Askelon;
Lest the daughters of the Philistines rejoice,
Lest the daughters of the uncircumcised triumph.

Ye mountains of Gilboa, let there be no dew, neither let there be rain upon you,

Nor fields of offerings:
  For there the shield of the mighty is vilely cast away,
  The shield of Saul as though he had not been anointed
    with oil.

From the blood of the slain,
From the fat of the mighty,
  The bow of Jonathan turned not back,
  And the sword of Saul returned not empty.

Saul and Jonathan were lovely and pleasant in their lives,
And in their death they were not divided;
  They were swifter than eagles,
  They were stronger than lions.

Ye daughters of Israel,
Weep over Saul,
  Who clothed you in scarlet with other delights,
  Who put on ornaments of gold upon your apparel.

How are the mighty—
Fallen in the midst of the battle!
  O Jonathan,
  Thou wast slain in thine high places.

I am distressed for thee, my brother Jonathan:
Very pleasant hast thou been unto me:
  Thy love to me was wonderful,
  Passing the love of women.

How are the mighty—
Fallen!
And the weapons of war—
Perished![1]

Saul accomplished a great deal for the people of Israel. Under his leadership they were definitely united into a nation. His great ability as a general taught them much about warfare and he proved to them that they were powerful enough to resist their

[1] II Samuel i, 19–27.

enemies, and though small, to be counted amongst the nations of the world. The two kings who followed Saul were both greater than he, but it was Saul who had successfully laid the foundations of a Hebrew kingdom upon which they were able to build.

David, the Hero-King of Israel

David was now acknowledged King of Israel. He had passed unharmed through many perils, temptations and difficulties, and his fame as a warrior together with his personal charm made him recognised as a leader of men, and the fittest person to be king. There were still, however, some who wanted one of Saul's sons to be king, and David was not allowed to take his kingdom without opposition. Abner, the chief captain of Saul's army, made an attempt to set one of Saul's sons on the throne, but he did not succeed and in a battle fought between him and the followers of David, he was beaten and forced to flee. Abner was pursued by Asahel, the brother of Joab, one of David's mighty men. He was "as light of foot as a wild roe," and soon overtook Abner, but when he had almost reached him, Abner turned round and fell upon Asahel and slew him. Later in the day, as the sun was going down, Joab and Abishai, the two brothers of Asahel, came to the place where he lay dead and they took up his body and buried him.

In the meantime Abner had gone to David in Hebron and made his peace with the king. But Joab and Abishai lay in wait for him and as he was returning from David, Joab treacherously slew him. When David heard what had happened, he was full of wrath towards Joab and Abishai. He declared that he was guiltless concerning the death of Abner who had been a great man in Israel, and that the responsibility for the cruel deed rested on the house of Joab.

All the first part of David's reign had to be given to making the kingdom sure for himself and the country secure from foreign foes. It was a hard task but he succeeded. He conquered Jerusalem, a strong city up in the hills and made it the capital of his kingdom.

Ever since the Ark had been restored to Israel by the Philistines, it had been kept in the house of Abinadab at Kirjath-jearim. In order to make the importance of Jerusalem as the principal city more sure, David decided to move the Ark to Jerusalem, where it was to be kept in a tent specially prepared for it.

The Ark was brought in a great procession to Jerusalem. Arrived at the gates of the city, a choir of priests demanded admission for it.

> Lift up your heads, O ye gates;
> And be ye lift up, ye everlasting doors,
> And the King of Glory shall come in.

And the warders within answered,

> Who is the King of Glory?

To which the priests replied,

> It is the Lord strong and mighty,
> Even the Lord mighty in battle.

And once again the priests demanded admission,

> Lift up your heads, O ye gates;
> And be ye lift up, ye everlasting doors,
> And the King of Glory shall come in.

And again the question,

> Who is the King of Glory?

And once again came the triumphant answer,

> Even the Lord of Hosts,
> He is the King of Glory.[1]

The Ark was admitted, and set up in the place that had been prepared for it, and a great festival of rejoicing was held. The Ark was to the Hebrew people a symbol of the Presence of God Himself, and the Ark was in Jerusalem.

At Jerusalem David held his court. One of his chief characteristics was the power he had of inspiring loyalty and affection in his friends and at Jerusalem he gathered round him a devoted band of warriors. David would now have liked to build a temple for the Ark. He felt it was not fitting that he should dwell in a more stately house than the Ark of God. But it was not he that should build it. The prophet brought him a message from God, who had said: "Thou shalt not build a house for my Name, because thou hast been a man of war and hast shed blood." It was to be Solomon his son who was to build it.

Not long after this, Israel was again at war with

[1] Psalm xxiv.

the Ammonites. Joab was in command of the army but David had remained behind at Jerusalem. Now there was in Jerusalem a man called Uriah, a Hittite, who had a very beautiful wife whose name was Bathsheba. And David loved Bathsheba and desired to have her for his wife. He called Uriah to him and bade him go as a messenger with a letter to Joab. The letter bade Joab set Uriah in the forefront of the battle that he might be killed. This was done and the news of his death was brought back to Jerusalem. When the days of her mourning for Uriah were over, David sent for Bathsheba and made her his wife. Then the prophet Nathan came to David and in a parable of great beauty he brought home to the king the shamefulness of the deed he had committed. And David acknowledged what he had done and humbled himself in real penitence before Jehovah.

Years went by, but as David grew older troubles came upon him. One of his best-loved sons was Absalom, a young man of great personal charm and beauty. To his father's great grief he rebelled against him and tried to make himself king. Absalom had a large number of followers. David was growing older and the youth and vigour of Absalom probably appealed to many of the young men. David was the first king to live in a royal palace in the city. Saul had led a soldier's life seldom away from a camp and there were doubtless many men of the old school who thought that David's manner of living was tending too much towards the luxury of the oriental monarchs. The rebellion grew so formidable that David was actually forced to flee from Jerusalem. In the end the rebellion was put down, but contrary to David's express command, Absalom was slain. This news nearly broke the heart of the old king. He loved his son so well that he would gladly have given his life for him. "Oh, my son Absalom," he lamented, "O Absalom, my son, my son! Would God I had died for thee, O Absalom, my son, my son!"

David now thought that he would like to number the people of Israel, but for doing this he was seriously reproved by the prophet Gad. It would seem that he had no particular purpose in this numbering, beyond a vainglorious desire to feel that he ruled over a large and prosperous kingdom.

And so the years went by. David grew very old and it was necessary that he should make some choice as to his successor. He was only the second king to reign over all Israel, and the custom that a man should succeed his father was not yet established. One of the ancient customs amongst certain Bedouin tribes of the East was that the dying chief should name the man he wished to succeed him. This custom was observed in the time of David, who named his son Solomon as his successor.

A great assembly of the people was called together and in solemn words David presented to them Solomon his son. He made an appeal to the people for gifts for the building of the house of the Lord which he charged Solomon to build, and then in moving words the aged king spoke to his son: "And thou, Solomon, my son, know thou the God of thy father, and serve Him with a perfect heart and with a willing mind: for the Lord searcheth all hearts, and understandeth all the imaginations of the thoughts; if thou seek Him, He will be found of thee; but if thou forsake Him, He will cast thee off for ever. Take heed now; for the Lord hath chosen thee to build an house for the sanctuary; be strong and do it."[1]

Great gifts were brought for the temple, of gold and silver and precious stones. There was great rejoicing. The country was at peace and prosperous and we are told that the people made their offerings willingly and in abundance. Then a great sacrifice was offered to Jehovah, and David offered the thanksgiving of his people. He said:

Blessed be Thou,
Lord God of Israel our Father,
for ever and ever.

Thine, O Lord,
is the greatness, and the power, and the glory,
and the victory, and the majesty:
for all that is in the heaven and in the earth
is Thine;
Thine is the Kingdom, O Lord,
and Thou art exalted as Head above all.

Both riches and honour come of Thee,
and Thou reignest over all;
and in Thine hand is power and might;
and in Thine hand it is to make great,
and to give strength unto all.

Now, therefore, our God,
we thank Thee,
and praise Thy glorious Name.

[1] I Chronicles xxviii, 9–10.

But who am I, and what is my people,
that we should be able to offer so willingly after this sort?
For all things come of Thee,
and of Thine own have we given Thee.[1]

Then David turning to the people said: "Now bless the Lord your God." And all the congregation blessed the Lord God of their fathers and bowed down their heads and worshipped the Lord.

David had reigned for forty years. He died in a good old age, full of days, riches and honour, and Solomon his son reigned in his stead.

David had all the qualities which make a leader of men. He was brave, chivalrous and generous. He loved his friends and inspired them with loyal devotion to himself. He was a far-famed warrior and at the same time a poet and musician. His character showed at its best in times of difficulty and danger; in prosperity and success he was sometimes weak in controlling his own desires, and as a father he was too indulgent and spoilt his children. But Israel owed great things to David. He built well on the foundations Saul had laid, and at his death the kingdom of Israel was in such a prosperous condition, that his son could devote his whole time to the occupations of peace without fear of invasion or of hostile attacks from neighbouring countries.

The deeds of David were sung throughout the succeeding centuries, and the Hebrews always looked back to him as their ideal king, their great national hero, one who was a "man after God's own heart."

[1] I Chronicles xxix, 10–14.

Solomon, the Builder

Solomon found himself ruler over a strong kingdom, secure from outside aggression and prosperous at home. He was only twenty years of age. He began his reign well, with the highest ideals, and with a prayer to Jehovah that he might have an "understanding heart to judge the people." Tradition has handed down his name as that of a man famed for his wisdom which was said to exceed that of Egypt, and for his proverbs and wise sayings, but he was also a king determined to make his country of more importance in the world than she had hitherto been.

Solomon first organised his kingdom and arranged his court, not on the simpler lines which had contented Saul and David, but more like that of other eastern kings of his time, which meant great splendour, magnificence and luxury. He made friends with other countries; he married an Egyptian princess, and made a trade alliance with the Phœnician king, Hiram of Tyre. He traded with many other countries, getting horses and chariots from Egypt, cedarwood from Lebanon, and gold, spices, sandalwood, apes, peacocks and ivory from the East. Though the Hebrews never became great sailors, Solomon built a navy which carried the trade of Israel to distant shores, according to tradition even as far as India.

Solomon was also a great builder. David had charged him to build a temple in which to keep the Ark and in which Jehovah might be worshipped, and he had begun to collect materials. Solomon now began to build and through his alliance with Hiram, King of Tyre, he was able to procure not only valuable building material but also skilled workmen in all kinds of metal-work, for which Tyre was famous, and weavers of beautiful fabrics from Sidon. Wealth, labour and time were lavished on the temple in order that it might be worthy of Jehovah. The site chosen was a piece of hilly ground in Jerusalem. The general plan was in many ways similar to that of the Tabernacle and not unlike that of an Egyptian temple. Through a porch one passed into the main body of the building, called the Holy Place, out of which opened an inner chamber known as the Holy of Holies. Two huge golden cherubim stood in this sanctuary; their wings were outstretched and the Ark was placed between them. Only the High Priest might enter there, and he only once a year.

When the temple was finished, a solemn festival of dedication was held. The Ark was set up in its place, and then Solomon knelt down before the altar and offered a prayer to Jehovah for his people.

O Lord God of Israel,
there is no God like Thee
in the heaven, nor in the earth;
which keepest covenant,
and showest mercy unto Thy servants,
that walk before Thee with all their hearts.

. . . .

Will God in very deed dwell with men on the earth?
Behold,

Heaven and the heaven of heavens cannot contain Thee;
How much less this house which I have built!

Have respect, therefore, to the prayer of Thy servant,
and to his supplication,
O Lord my God,
To hearken unto the cry and the prayer
Which Thy servant prayeth before Thee:

That Thine eyes may be open upon this House
day and night,
Upon the place whereof Thou hast said
That Thou wouldest put Thy Name there;
To hearken unto the prayer
Which Thy servant prayeth toward this place.

Hearken therefore
Unto the supplications of Thy servant,
And of Thy people Israel,
Which they shall make towards this place:
Hear Thou
From heaven Thy dwelling-place,
even from heaven;
And when Thou hearest, forgive.

. . . .

Now therefore arise, O Lord God, into Thy resting place,
Thou, and the ark of Thy strength:
Let Thy priests, O Lord God, be clothed with salvation,
And let Thy saints rejoice in goodness.
O Lord God, turn not away the face of Thine anointed:
Remember David Thy servant.[1]

Solomon next built a palace for himself near the temple, but a little lower down the hill. It contained a hall, known as the House of the Forest of Lebanon, because of its forty-five large pillars made of cedar from Lebanon, a throne-room in which was the king's seat made of ivory and covered

[1] Chronicles vi, 14, 18–21, 41–42.

with gold, and the private apartments of the king and the queen.

Solomon's buildings did not stop with those at Jerusalem. He also built a chain of fortresses which guarded the frontiers of the kingdom, and he strengthened the defences of a number of towns.

The fame of Solomon spread far and wide and brought him many visitors. One of them was the Queen of Sheba. In eastern fashion she brought with her rich gifts of spices and gold and precious stones, but rich as she was herself, the splendour of Solomon's court amazed her and she declared that the half of it had not been told her.

But all these enterprises required money and large numbers of workmen. To obtain these Solomon was obliged to tax the people heavily, and to force men to work for him. This caused great discontent in the country, but his love of luxury and magnificence shut his eyes to the feeling in the land and made him more and more of a tyrant. As far as his resources permitted, he tried to imitate the splendours of the Egyptian and Babylonian courts, and these foreign influences caused him to forget Jehovah and to turn to strange gods. His heart was not perfect with the Lord his God as was the heart of David his father. As a result of all this Solomon gradually lost the affection and loyalty of his subjects, and at his death the country was in such a state of discontent that his son found open rebellion awaiting him.

CHAPTER IX

REBELLION AND THE DIVISION OF THE KINGDOM

It was the Hebrew custom that a king could not consider himself firmly established on the throne until he had been acknowledged king by his subjects. It was not sufficient that he should be the son or the choice of the former king, he must also be the choice of the people.

Solomon was followed by his son Rehoboam, but before the tribes in the north would recognize him as king, they asked him to promise that he would change his father's policy of heavy taxation and forced labour. If he would do this, they assured him of their loyal support. The northern tribes were led by Jeroboam, a young man of ability, who was a "mighty man of valour" and had qualities of leadership. The old and experienced men in the country, men who had not only served his father Solomon but had also known and loved his grandfather David, advised the young king to listen to these requests and to grant them. But Rehoboam, who knew nothing of the real conditions in the country and would probably not have cared much if he had known them, turned away from these wise counsellors, and listened instead to the foolish advice of the young men who had grown up with him. He not only absolutely refused to lighten any of the burdens his father had laid on the people, but he de-

CHART I

B. C.	EGYPT	MESOPOTAMIA, SYRIA and PERSIA	HEBREWS	GREECE	ROME	OTHER PARTS of the WORLD
3000—2000	Pyramid Builders 	Sumerian Civilization  SARGON, Founder of Empire in Western Asia				Early Aegean Civilization 
2000—1250	Egyptian Empire THUTMOSE III IKHNATON 	HAMMURABI 	ABRAHAM Hebrews in Egypt 			Hittite Empire Golden Age of Crete (Knossos)
1250—1050	RAMSES II MERNEPTAH		MOSES The Exodus In the Wilderness Conquest of Canaan JOSHUA Judges in Israel 			Phoenician Colonization 
1050—1000		 Assyrian Empire	SAUL DAVID SAMUEL NATHAN	Trojan War 		
10th Century			SOLOMON Division of the Kingdom Judah: REHOBOAM Israel: JEROBOAM I			HIRAM, King of Tyre

clared his intention of making them yet harder if he saw fit.

The result of this stupid answer was a rebellion against Rehoboam in the north. In the hope of putting it down he sent a messenger to treat with the northern tribes, but instead of sending some one who would have commanded their respect, he sent Adoram, the official who "was over the tribute," the man in charge of the hated taxation. When he arrived he was seized by the people and stoned to death.

The rebellion was successful and as a result the northern tribes separated from the southern and made themselves into an independent state, known as the Kingdom of Israel. The southern tribes were known henceforth as the Kingdom of Judah.

This division of the kingdom was a very important event in Hebrew history. It practically wrecked the work of Saul and David, for instead of one strong little kingdom there were now two weaker ones, constantly defending their land from foreign foes and often fighting each other. Disunited they were at last to fall before the might of Assyria and Babylon and cease to exist as independent nations.

CHAPTER X

HOW MEN LIVED IN ISRAEL UNDER THE KINGS

THE period of the kings brought a change not only in the administration of the land of Israel but also in the manner of living. There were still shepherds in the land and agriculture was still widely practised, but city-life now began to grow in importance.

Saul, the first king, had been a soldier living in camp, and during his reign the royal court had been a very simple one. Under David there was more formality, especially after he had made Jerusalem the capital. The king himself was both the supreme general and the supreme judge in Israel, but he had also officers and ministers to assist him.

The principal military leader under him was known as the Captain of the Host, and the host was a citizen army called whenever there was war. The chief ministers of the king were the Recorder, a man of high rank and distinction who stood very near the king, the Scribe or royal Secretary, also an official of great importance and dignity, and the Head of the Tribute whose business it was to see that the taxes were paid. There was little or no taxation during the reign of David, but from the time of Solomon onwards taxation, either in the form of money or in produce of the land, was regularly and sometimes oppressively exacted. Besides the regular taxation, the king obtained money in the form of tribute from conquered states, and all who visited the king brought gifts, the usual custom for guests in the East. Sometimes these gifts were of great value, like those brought to Solomon by the Queen of Sheba: "And she gave the king an hundred and twenty talents of gold, and of spices very great store, and precious stones: there came no more such abundance of spices as these which the Queen of Sheba gave to King Solomon."

In the Hebrew family the father was the most important person, and not only his slaves, but his wife and children were looked upon as his possessions. This did not mean that they were harshly treated, and the stories of Isaac and Rebekah, Jacob and Rachel, Elkanah and Hannah, show that the wife was treated more as an equal than a slave.

The name given to a child was of great importance. Its meaning was held as a symbol, sometimes of the circumstances under which he had been born, as Samuel, or of some event connected with him, as Moses; sometimes it was held to be a symbol of his character, as Jacob. Children were strictly brought up. "It is good for a man that he bear the yoke in his youth," said the prophet, and the rod was not spared.

Slaves in Israel were well treated on the whole. They could inherit their master's property if he had no heir, and the law emphasised the rights of slaves. A runaway slave was to be protected, and one of the reasons why the Sabbath was to be observed was that the slaves might rest: "The seventh day is the sabbath of the Lord thy God: in it thou shalt not do any work, thou, nor thy son, nor thy daughter, nor thy manservant, nor thy maidservant, nor thine ox, nor thine ass, nor any of thy cattle, nor thy stranger that is within thy gates; that thy manservant and thy maidservant may rest as well as thou."[1]

In early Israel justice had been administered by the village elders. During the monarchy this same system was observed, but appeals could be made to the king as supreme judge. From the large place in the Hebrew law occupied by the question of justice between man and man, it would seem that the Hebrews were constantly disputing with one another. The court of justice was held every morning at the gate of the city, and the accused had to prove his innocence, not always easy, no matter how innocent he was. For ordinary offences beating with rods was the punishment; when death was the penalty, the convicted man was stoned to death.

Country life both in Israel and Judah was a hard one. The village life was simple; the women did the spinning and weaving, they fetched the water from the well, they ground the corn. The men were either shepherds or farmers. The life of the farmer was one of hard work. He cultivated wheat and barley, the vine, olive and fig, and it was his ideal to be able to sit in safety under his own vine and fig-tree.

The shepherd and his flock was one of the most characteristic sights of the country, and allusions to the life and character of the good shepherd are con-

[1]Deuteronomy v, 14.

stantly found in the Old Testament. It was a life that called for rare courage and strength. David describing his life to Saul, said: "Thy servant kept his father's sheep, and there came a lion, and a bear, and took a lamb out of the flock: and I went out after him, and smote him, and delivered it out of his mouth; and when he arose against me, I caught him by his beard, and smote him and slew him. Thy servant slew both the lion and the bear."[1]

Jacob showed the care a shepherd gives to his flock when he said to Esau: "My lord knoweth that the flocks and herds with young are with me; and if men should overdrive them one day, all the flock will die."[2]

The prophets, too, knew what a good shepherd was like. "He shall feed his flock like a shepherd; he shall gather the lambs with his arm, and carry them in his bosom, and shall gently lead those that are with young."[3] "I will feed my flock, and I will cause them to lie down, saith the Lord God. I will seek that which was lost, and bring again that which was driven away, and will bind up that which was broken, and will strengthen that which was sick."[4]

From the time of David onwards, city-life became more important. Jerusalem became the home of the king, the headquarters of his body-guard, and of the chief ministers. The building of the temple and of the royal palace brought all kinds of craftsmen to Jerusalem, and later, Samaria became

[1] I Samuel xvii, 34–36.
[2] Genesis xxxiii, 13.
[3] Isaiah xl, 11.
[4] Ezekiel xxxiv, 15–16.

important as the capital of the northern kingdom of Israel.

The houses were small, they generally faced north and were built close together so as to get as much shade from the summer sun as possible. The roof was flat, and it was perhaps the most important part of the house. It commanded the best view over the city, it was the best place in which to get the cool air of the evening, it was on the roof that quiet could be obtained when the master of the house wished to be undisturbed, it was on the roof that he most often prayed. The roof was used so much that the law required that it should be protected by a balustrade: "When thou buildest a new house, then thou shalt make a battlement for thy roof, that thou bring not blood upon thy house, if any man fall from thence."[1]

The earliest houses were simple. The guest chamber in the house of the Shunammite held a bed, a table, a stool and a candlestick, but later the houses became larger and more luxurious. Amos complained of the growing luxury and of the "beds of ivory and couches" that were becoming the fashion.

As the houses grew more luxurious, so did the clothing. The long tunic-like garment reaching to the feet was still the chief garment, and over it was worn a cloak. This garment was more than a cloak, it served also as a blanket and sometimes as a carpet. So fully was this use of it recognised that the law required that had it been taken in pledge from a poor man, it should be returned to him at night-

[1]Deuteronomy xxii, 8.

time. "If thou at all take thy neighbour's raiment to pledge, thou shalt deliver it unto him by that the sun goeth down: for that is his covering only, it is his raiment for his skin: wherein shall he sleep?"[1] These garments were often richly embroidered. "Have they not sped? have they not divided the prey? to every man a damsel or two; to Sisera a prey of divers colours, a prey of divers colours of needlework, of divers colours of needlework on both sides, meet for the necks of them that take the spoil?"[2]

In the time of Solomon the clothing of his attendants was so magnificent that it called forth the admiration of the Queen of Sheba. A girdle was always worn to fasten the tunic, and it was frequently embroidered and ornamented with gold. The girdle was used for all kinds of purposes: the warrior fastened his sword in it, the scribe carried his writing there, women used it as a bag.

The prophets never had good words for city-life, not only those who lived in the desert and the country, but also those who, like Isaiah, were town-bred. Isaiah made many protests against the increasing luxury and love of display of the women and he gives a list of the ornaments and garments worn by the women of Jerusalem. To him they were symbols of heartless extravagance. He describes how they "walk, mincing as they go, and make a tinkling with their feet," and he goes on to speak of "the chains, and the bracelets, and the mufflers, the bonnets, and the ornaments of the legs, and the head-

[1]Exodus xxii, 26–27. [2]Judges v, 30.

bands, and the tablets, and the earrings, the rings and nose jewels, the changeable suits of apparel, and the mantles, and the wimples, and the crisping pins, the glasses, and the fine linen, and the hoods, and the veils."[1]

Foreign influence was clearly marked in these ornaments. The chief native crafts of the Hebrews were those of the builder and carpenter, the potter, dyer, cloth-maker and metal-worker. Much of this they had learnt from their neighbours, and many of the articles of luxury they required had to be imported. From the time of Solomon onwards there was a good deal of commerce between Israel and her neighbours, the chief exports being oil, honey, nuts, almonds, figs and wheat.

On the whole, the food of the ancient Hebrew was simple: flour, honey, oil, vegetables, fruit, certain kinds of meat. But during the monarchy good living became more general. The court of Solomon required a good deal of food each day: "And Solomon's provision for one day was thirty measures of fine flour, and threescore measures of meal, ten fat oxen, and twenty oxen out of the pastures, and an hundred sheep, besides harts, and roebucks, and fallow deer, and fatted fowl."[2]

To the ancient Hebrew the eating of a meal with another was a symbolic act, to which he attached great importance. It meant to him that those who had joined in a common meal had established a relationship of friendliness and good-will each to the other.

[1]Isaiah iii, 19–23. [2]I Kings iv, 22–23.

The Hebrew had inherited the virtue of hospitality from his Bedouin ancestors. When Abraham entertained the young men, whom he afterwards recognised as angels, unawares, he did it with all the graciousness of those who dwell in tents in a desert land. The slave upon his master's business was entertained with courtesy and consideration both for himself and for his beasts. The daughters of the priest of Midian were reproved by their father for not having immediately brought to his tent Moses, the stranger who had given them timely and kindly help, in order that he might eat bread with them. And of all the stories of eastern hospitality of which the Old Testament is so full, perhaps none shows more gracious tact and kindly courtesy and consideration than that of the Shunammite who planned the prophet's chamber, to which Elisha might come and go, unquestioned and undisturbed, but knowing that he was a welcome and much loved and reverenced guest in the house of friends.

The centre of the life of the city was at the gate. It was there that justice was administered, meetings were held, bargains made, the latest news discussed. Job describes the respect in which the elders of the city were held when they came to give their judgments at the gate: "When I went out to the gate through the city, when I prepared my seat in the street, the young men saw me, and hid themselves: and the aged arose, and stood up. The princes refrained talking, and laid their hand on their mouth. The nobles held their peace, and their tongue cleaved to the roof of their mouth. Unto me men gave ear, and waited, and kept silence at my counsel."

And he goes on to describe the kind of judgment that was given by an upright judge:

When the ear heard me, then it blessed me;
And when the eye saw me, it gave witness to me:
Because I delivered the poor that cried,
And the fatherless, and him that had none to help him.
The blessing of him that was ready to perish came upon
me:
And I caused the widow's heart to sing for joy.
I put on righteousness, and it clothed me:
My judgment was as a robe and a diadem.
I was eyes to the blind,
And feet was I to the lame.
I was a father to the poor:
And the cause which I knew not I searched out.[1]

The East has always plenty of time, and the meeting of acquaintances in the street was an occasion of much ceremony and formal salutation. But even for the East it sometimes took up too much time. Hurried messengers had to be instructed that if they met any one he was not to be saluted, neither were they to return a salutation. But this was only on occasions when haste was necessary. The ordinary words of greeting and farewell were "Peace be with thee," "The Lord be with thee," and though doubtless the words became as formal and careless and forgetful of their real meaning as the English word "Goodbye," they yet held within them, even as does the English word, the grace and courtesy of an ancient benediction.

[1]Job xxix, 7–16.

CHAPTER XI

KINGS IN ISRAEL FROM JEROBOAM TO JEHU

THE rebellion against Rehoboam had established the independent kingdom of Israel in the north and Jeroboam had become king. The first thing he did was to make Shechem the chief city, but it was found difficult to defend against attacks from enemies, and later on Samaria took its place as the capital of Israel.

Jeroboam was a popular leader and an able king, but he did not belong to the family of David. However tyrannical Rehoboam might be, people remembered that he was the grandson of David, the Hero-King. Jeroboam was afraid that if the people of the north continued going to the yearly feasts at Jerusalem, something of the glamour of the house of David would capture their imagination and he might lose their loyalty and allegiance. To prevent this he set up two calves of gold, one at Bethel and one at Dan, with priests to sacrifice at the altars. He said to the people: "It is too much for you to go up to Jerusalem: behold thy gods, O Israel, which brought thee up out of the land of Egypt."

Jeroboam was bitterly blamed by the ancient Hebrew writers for having set up these sanctuaries in which there were calves of gold to be worshipped. He does not seem, however, to have intended the calves to be *idols,* but *symbols* of the strength of Jehovah. Jeroboam was breaking the second rather than the first commandment and he was probably moved more by political than by religious reasons. But this compromise with wrong in order that he might keep his own power was to bring evil consequences upon his people, for later on it made the way only too easy for them to fall into idolatry.

Jeroboam had other difficulties during his reign. There were wars with the southern kingdom of Judah and probably with both the Philistines and Egypt, but he kept the kingdom together and after a reign of twenty-two years handed it over to his son Nadab.

For about twenty-five years after the death of Jeroboam the kingdom of Israel was ruled by a succession of warlike kings. It was a time of great unrest. Nadab ruled for two years and then a conspiracy was formed against him by Baasha, who slew him and every one belonging to the house of Jeroboam whom he could find, and then reigned as king in his stead. Baasha fought with Asa, King of Judah, and pressed him hard, but he was unable to conquer him, and after twelve years he left the kingdom to his son. Two years later, this son was murdered by one of his captains, Zimri, who reigned as king for seven days. Then the people turned against the usurper and supported Omri, the captain of the host, and him they made king.

Omri was a strong king. It was he who made Samaria the capital. He restored order to the land torn with anarchy, and he seems to have made peace with the neighbouring kings, especially with those of Assyria and Syria, though at the price of paying heavy tribute to them. But he kept the sanctuaries set up by Jeroboam and made no effort to restrain his people from falling into idolatry. He reigned for six years and was then succeeded by his son Ahab.

Under Ahab there began a period of greater prosperity for Israel than she had yet enjoyed. The northern kingdom was more prosperous than the southern kingdom of Judah. Samaria was now the capital and it soon became a flourishing city. Trade increased with Damascus and over the great roads to Egypt. Towns grew larger and better houses were built, but it was the rich who prospered, and their prosperity was gained at the expense of the poor, who laboured and paid heavy taxes that the rich might live in luxury. Intercourse with neighbouring countries brought an introduction of the worship of false gods into Israel, and all kinds of idolatry were soon practiced by the people.

Ahab did a good deal to increase the intercourse of Israel with her neighbours. In the first place, he married Jezebel, a Phœnician princess, a woman of ability, of fanatic religious zeal, and thoroughly determined to use any means, no matter how wicked, to carry out her own personal wishes. She was a worshipper of the Phœnician god Baal, and she set up a temple served by a large number of priests to this heathen god. Then Ahab married his daughter Athaliah to Jehoram, son of Jehoshaphat, king of Judah, and so made an alliance with the southern kingdom.

Omri, the father of Ahab, had secured peace with

Syria by paying a heavy tribute. Ahab began by continuing this payment, but this did not content the Syrian king, Ben-hadad, who sent messengers to Ahab demanding the payment of a still greater sum. Ahab had been willing to pay a reasonable amount, but he considered this demand excessive, and sent back a sharp refusal. War was the result and there followed a great battle in which Ben-hadad was defeated. But Ahab did not put him to death. He was set free and allowed to return to his own land on condition that he restore to Israel the cities his father had captured and that certain streets in Damascus should be given over to Israelite traders and merchants.

Encouraged by his success against Ben-hadad and by the sense of security his policy and alliances were giving him, Ahab seems to have thought that nothing could be denied him. Just at this time he set his heart on acquiring a vineyard which was close to the royal palace in Samaria. This vineyard belonged to Naboth of Jezreel and Ahab offered to buy it from him. But the vineyard was a family inheritance of Naboth's and he refused to part with it. Jezebel, a very much stronger character than Ahab, taunted him with not being king in his own land, and she contrived a plot whereby Naboth was accused before the elders of his city of blaspheming against God and the king. There seems to have been no real trial. Naboth was condemned on the word of paid false witnesses, taken out and stoned to death, the Hebrew punishment for blasphemy.

Now the prophet Elijah heard of what had been

done to Naboth, and he went to Ahab and denounced him for that cruel and unjust deed and for other evil deeds he and Jezebel, his wife, had committed. He told him that his descendants should not reign after him, but that his family should become like that of Jeroboam and Baasha and that Jezebel, his wife, should share their fate.

There was now peace for three years between Israel and Syria and then war broke out again. Ramoth-gilead was an important town east of the Jordan on the highroad from Damascus to the Red Sea. It had originally belonged to Israel, but it had been captured by Syria in the days of Omri, and was one of the cities Ben-hadad had promised to return to Israel. Syria was now trying to get back Ramoth-gilead and Ahab determined on war to settle the matter. He was still allied with Judah, and he asked the king, Jehoshaphat, if he would join him and so make more certain the defeat of Syria. Jehoshaphat consented, but according to the ancient custom, asked Ahab to consult the prophets of Jehovah as to how the war would end. Ahab sent for the prophets he had gathered about him—we are told there were four hundred of them—and asked whether he should go against Ramoth-gilead or not. With one voice they answered, "Go up; for the Lord shall deliver it into the hand of the king."

But Jehoshaphat was not satisfied; perhaps he doubted the sincerity of these men and wondered if they were in the pay of the king, and he asked if there were no other prophet in the land besides these men. Ahab told him there was Micaiah who might be consulted, but he added, "I hate him, for he doth not prophesy good concerning me, but evil." In spite of this answer, Jehoshaphat asked that he might be summoned. He came, and then there followed a dramatic scene: the two kings on their thrones, clad in robes of state; the four hundred prophets obsequiously prophesying success to the king in whose pay they were and who was willing to sacrifice even his religion and his honour, if it would procure him the assistance he wanted from the king of Judah; and Micaiah, alone, unpopular, determined to speak the truth at all costs. He foretold disaster and denounced the lying prophets who had attempted to deceive the king.

In spite, however, of Micaiah's prophecy the two kings went out to battle. Ahab disguised himself as an ordinary soldier, but Jehoshaphat went out to the battle with all the pomp that surrounded eastern kings. The king of Syria had given orders that every effort was to be made to capture or kill the king of Israel. When his captains saw Jehoshaphat, thinking this must be the king of Israel they surrounded his chariot, but he called out to them that he was not Ahab and they turned aside and left him. Then it came about that a certain archer, drawing a bow at random, shot an arrow which pierced the heart of Ahab, and his servants, seeing him fall, came hastily and took him out of the battle. He died at even, and they brought his body to Samaria where they buried him.

Ahab had been an energetic and in many ways an able king, but he had disregarded all the nobler ideals of his people and he had ruled like a tyrant, with the result that under the two weak kings who succeeded him, there was confusion and anarchy. Then it was that Elisha the prophet encouraged Jehu, one of the captains of the host, to head a revolt and become king. He sent a messenger to Ramoth-gilead where Jehu was with the army, with instructions to anoint him as king. This was done and then, in true eastern fashion, the messenger went on to tell him that he was to destroy all who belonged to the house of Ahab. When he had delivered his message, the man opened the door and fled. The friends of Jehu acclaimed him immediately, placed him on a hastily improvised throne and blew trumpets, crying out: "Jehu is king! Jehu is king!"

In this way Jehu the son of Nimshi conspired against the king of Israel. He gave orders that no one was to leave Ramoth-gilead with the news, but he himself set out alone for Jezreel, where the king of Israel was. And then follows a grim tale of ruthless butchery. Jehu, driving furiously in his chariot, reached Jezreel. The king came out to meet him, asking if he came in peace. For answer Jehu drew a bow with his full strength and the king sank back dead. Jehu went on into the city, and looking up at a window saw Jezebel gazing out. Dressed in all the painted splendour of an oriental, fearless and proud, she looked down on Jehu and taunted him: "Had Zimri peace who slew his master?" But grimly Jehu gave orders to throw her out of the window and kill her. It was done and as Jehu went on his way, he drove over her body. Later in the day, however, he seems to have had some compunction, and he gave orders that she should be buried for, he said, "she is a king's daughter."

Jehu did not rest until the house of Ahab had been wiped off the face of the earth, but even when that had been done there were still the prophets and worshippers of Baal in the land. Jehu resolved to purge Israel of the idolatry introduced by Jezebel and announcing that if Ahab served Baal little, Jehu should serve him much, he gathered together a great assembly of Baal worshippers as for a festival. Then, when they were assembled, he sent his soldiers into their midst, and the whole company was slain.

In the history of the Hebrew people up to this time there had been many a deed of cruelty performed, as was believed, at the command of Jehovah, but never had there been quite such an appalling horror as this vengeance of Jehu on the house of Ahab. Yet the Hebrew writer justified it and believed it was in accordance with the will of Jehovah, and Elisha who had sent his own disciple to anoint Jehu, does not appear to have lifted up his voice in protest. It is true that the times were cruel, and that Assyria, that most bloodthirsty of all empires, was at the height of her power and was showing the ancient world how she dealt with her enemies. But not even Assyria did anything much worse than these deeds of Jehu. All that can be said, not in justification, but in explanation, is that the people of Israel regarded Jehovah as their

King, the Lord of Hosts, stern, and demanding nothing less than what an earthly king demanded, the extermination of his enemies. They believed that disloyalty to Him was treason, the punishment of which was death. They had not yet learnt that Jehovah was a God of Mercy and Love. The conception of God, of all that He is, is something that is beyond our finite human minds. Different ages have had different conceptions, based chiefly on the ideals of what is noblest and most exalted that are cherished by each age. In the ninth century B.C. the vision of the Conqueror with his foot on the neck of his captive ordering the extermination of his enemies was universally admired. Another hundred years were to pass before the conception of Jehovah as a God who loved mercy was to be put very clearly before the people, and when that time came, the prophet makes it clear that these very deeds of Jehu were deeds of which the nation should be ashamed.

We know very little more of what Jehu did, and that little comes from Assyrian records. He seems to have paid tribute to the king of Assyria and to have bought peace with the Assyrians at the price of vessels of gold and silver. We are told that he reigned for twenty-eight years and that when he died, he was buried, like Ahab, in the royal city of Samaria.

CHAPTER XII

THE HEBREW PROPHET

The Prophet

THE first great change in the history of the Hebrews took place after their conquest of Canaan, when from being nomad tribes they became a settled agricultural people. The second change took place when their town life developed, when to the life of the husbandman they added that of the merchant and trader. This town life was more fully developed in the northern kingdom of Israel, but Judah also came under its influence. During this period there arose great teachers of the people, who were known as Prophets.

The name "prophet" is often only given to one who foretells the future, but the title as it was given to the Hebrew prophets means a great deal more than this. The real meaning of the word "prophet" is "one who speaks on behalf of another," and the Hebrew prophets spoke to the people on behalf of Jehovah. They made known to them the will and character of Jehovah; they explained as far as they understood what the various events of their history meant, and what the nation might expect as a result; they gave them their religious teaching; they pointed out their dangers, and warned them against forgetting Jehovah and giving way to idolatry like the nations round them. As the Hebrews grew in wealth and developed a higher civilisation, the temptations beset them that beset all wealthy and civilised communities; the rich wanted to grow richer, and so the poor were oppressed; money was spent on self-gratification instead of for the good of the whole community.

The early simple relationship of the Hebrews to Jehovah had now disappeared, and they no longer thought of Him as their God who took a close personal interest in their affairs. They worshipped Him with great ceremonies in the temple, but He was far away from them, they did not *know* Him. Their strength was in their prosperity, not in their religion. One of their wise men once said: "Where there is no vision, the people perish," and it was at a time when they were in danger of perishing for lack of a vision that there arose the great Hebrew prophets who placed one before them. We know very little about the lives of the prophets themselves, for in the records that have been left us, the work and service of a prophet for the people have been considered of greater importance than the life of the man himself. But their personality shines through their words, and though we know but little of the events of their lives we have a clear picture of their character.

The prophets were great patriots as well as great religious teachers, and they took an important part in the life of the nation. Their eyes were on the future, and they awoke in the people a desire for better conditions than those of their very troubled present. They set up ideals of righteousness and justice not only for Israel but for the world. But the prophets were not dreamers of idle dreams, they were practical men, well-informed as to the conditions of their day, but they believed that such things as they preached were possible, and part of their work was to make the people share their belief, for unfaltering faith in the ultimate triumph of an idea is a great factor in bringing about its fulfilment.

The Forerunners: Elijah and Elisha

The forerunner of the great prophets was Elijah. Nothing is known of his early life, except that he came from the desert. He lived during the reign of Ahab, king of Israel. Dressed in the rough mantle of a shepherd and carrying a shepherd's staff, he would appear suddenly in the midst of the king and people denouncing their idolatry. He was a very striking and dramatic figure. His early life in the desert had taught him to bear hardships easily and had accustomed him to take long journeys on foot, so that he used to appear and disappear and then appear again before the king and people with unexpected and startling rapidity.

We know very little of what Elijah did between his sudden appearances. Once he was hiding from the angry king by a brook, and ravens brought him food; on another occasion he visited a poor widow who shared her scanty fare with him. Then in the presence of Ahab he had a great public contest on Mount Carmel with the prophets of Baal in order to prove to the people which was the true God of

Israel. Weak and wavering in their belief they had seemed uncertain whether to give their allegiance to Jehovah or to Baal. "How long halt ye between two opinions?" cried Elijah, "if the Lord be God, follow Him; but if Baal, follow him." The contest lasted all day, it is one of the most dramatic stories in the Old Testament. It ended in a complete victory for Elijah and as the hour of the evening sacrifice drew near, the people fell on their faces and said: "The Lord, he is the God; the Lord, he is the God!"

When Ahab returned to his palace and told Jezebel the queen, who had been chiefly responsible for the introduction of the Baal worship into Israel, what had happened, she was very angry and determined that Elijah should be put to death.

Elijah had gained a great triumph on Mount Carmel, but now, forced to hide from the vindictive anger of the queen, his courage forsook him and lonely and discouraged he wished that he might die. As he hid in a cave, a great and strong wind arose that rent the mountains and broke the rocks in pieces, and the earth trembled beneath an earthquake and fire, and then there was silence. And through the silence came the voice of Jehovah to Elijah bidding him play the man and take heart and go back and work. He was to anoint a man called Elisha to succeed him as prophet in Israel, and above all he was to remember that not all in Israel had forsaken Jehovah.

Elijah went back to his work and again and yet again he denounced the idolatry of the king. And then, as he had appeared, so he disappeared, suddenly, taken up to heaven according to the old tradition by a whirlwind in a chariot of fire with horses of fire.

Elijah was very stern and uncompromising. To him, as to Moses, Jehovah was the God of the Hebrews, and every inclination to idolatry was to be stamped out, but he believed that other nations might worship other gods, so long as Israel remained faithful. To him, Jehovah was the Lord of Hosts, who would punish all wickedness, but who would save Israel and triumph over the gods of the heathen.

Elisha was a very different man from Elijah, whose mantle, we are told, had fallen upon him. He could be stern and pitiless when necessary, but he had a gentler and more gracious personality than his master. Elijah seems to have preferred the loneliness and austerity of the desert for a dwelling-place, Elisha was happier in towns and with his fellowmen. Elijah had great moments of vision and inspiration, but he also experienced the desolation of spirit that comes to austere and lonely souls. Elisha, on the other hand, had a more even temperament, and most of the stories we know of him show him going about doing kindly and gentle acts of mercy.

Of all the stories of Elisha, perhaps that which shows his kindliness at its best is the story of the Shunammite and her son. This was the story of the rich lady of Shunem who had added the Prophet's Chamber to her house. A little son was born to her, and as he grew up into boyhood he loved to be with his father in the fields. But one hot day when he went out, he was struck down by the hot sun and carried home unconscious and in a few hours he died. Then the lady of Shunem sent in haste to Elisha, who came to her and restored her child to life and health.

The fame of Elisha spread beyond the borders of Israel, and he became known in Damascus as well as in Samaria. We are told the story of how Naaman, the captain of the host of the king of Syria, was smitten with leprosy, and of how in far-off Damascus, the little Israelitish maid who had been taken captive in one of the wars and was serving the wife of Naaman, persuaded her master to go to Elisha the prophet for healing. And he went, and was healed.

CHAPTER XIII

THE FALL OF NORTHERN ISRAEL

The Prophets: Amos and Hosea

THE first of the prophets whose writings we have is Amos, who lived more than a hundred years after Elijah.

Amos taught in northern Israel at a time of great outward prosperity. Samaria had become a very flourishing city and trade had increased with neighbouring countries. "There were palaces of ivory in Samaria, and houses of hewn stone without number, castles and forts, horses and chariots, power and pomp, splendour and riches, wherever one might turn. The rich lay on couches of ivory with damask cushions; daily they slew the fatted calf, drank the most costly wines, and anointed themselves with precious oils."[1] But all this prosperity was gained at the expense of the poor, who laboured and paid heavy taxes that the rich might live in this luxury, which meant that the prosperity was built on an unsound foundation and was not likely to last.

Religious matters were in an equally dangerous condition. Israel was believing that outward wealth and prosperity were a sign of the reward of virtue and of the special favour of Jehovah, and that the worship the most pleasing to Him was that of state-

[1]Quoted from Cornill, "The Prophets of Israel."

ly outward ceremony and magnificence. The most serious result of this was that in the religion of Israel emphasis was not placed on right conduct, and that outward observances were taking the place of good deeds.

Into this way of living and worshipping came Amos. He was a herdsman and his early life had been a simple one, spent away from cities. At some time he must have travelled about a good deal, probably in order to sell his wool, for he seems to have known all about the conditions in different parts of the country. He first appeared in public at Bethel on a feast-day. Like Elijah he appeared, delivered his message, and then for a time disappeared again.

The vision of Amos was the widest that the Hebrews had yet had placed before them, for he broke away from the old idea that Jehovah was the God of one nation only, and he taught that He was the God of the whole earth. He reminded the people of much of their early history, and entreated them to give up the idolatry into which they had fallen, and their injustice and oppression of the poor.

Amos put two new ideas before Israel: that privileges given to people meant opportunities of service and responsibilities for using them, and that good acts were better than elaborate ceremonies. He told Israel that Jehovah cared nothing for rites and ceremonies, no matter how splendidly they were carried out, if they were not based on character and did not go hand in hand with righteous deeds.

This teaching went a great deal further than the harsh laws Moses had been obliged to make for the ignorant and undisciplined people he had in his care. His work and that of the earlier teachers and prophets had been to impress upon Israel that Jehovah was their *God:* the work of Amos and of those who came after him was to make known the *character* of Jehovah and what He required from those who believed in Him.

It was not easy for Israel to accept the teaching that Jehovah was the God of the whole world. Hitherto they had looked on Him as the God of their own nation and on themselves as His chosen people, and they were jealous and unwilling to acknowledge that His sovereignty was over others as well. Yet this was not the whole teaching of Amos. Jehovah, he taught, was the God of the whole world, nevertheless Israel was right in calling herself the chosen people, for Jehovah had chosen her from out of the nations of the ancient world to be His witness and to do His work. But in spite of the repeated forgiveness of Jehovah for her many crimes, Israel had proved faithless to Him who had called her, and so Amos declared that Jehovah would break her and make her "high hills low and her greatness as dust." Israel was to fall, yet out of her seeming defeat was to come the victory of the Justice and Righteousness of Jehovah.

The successor of Amos as prophet in Israel was Hosea. Amos had left as his message that war and the bitterness of captivity would be the fate of the people of Israel. He had said to them, "Seek ye the

Lord and ye shall live," but from much of what he taught, it is evident that he believed that the patience of Jehovah was exhausted, and that whatever hope there was for Israel was for a future and not his own generation. Yet at the same time as this belief in the sternness of Jehovah there was in Israel a growing belief in His mercy and love. It was His "ancient gentleness with them which had made them great," and throughout their long and troubled history His tenderness and graciousness had watched over them.

> He found him in a desert land.
> And in the waste howling wilderness;
> He compassed him about, he cared for him.
> He kept him as the apple of his eye:
> As an eagle that stirreth up her nest,
> That fluttereth over her young,
> He spread abroad his wings, he took them,
> He bare them on his pinions:
> So Jehovah alone did lead him.[1]

It was the prophet Hosea who first showed Israel that this ancient Love of Jehovah was even greater than His Law and Justice and Righteousness. The standards of Hosea were no less high than those of Amos, and he, too, believed that disaster and ruin awaited Israel in the immediate future, but he also believed that there would come a future when Israel, purified and redeemed through suffering, would return to Jehovah. Alone amongst the nations of the ancient world, Israel looked forward instead of back. To the Hebrews the Golden Age lay

[1]Deuteronomy xxxii, 10–12, R. V.

in the future and not in the past, and of all their teachers, none taught the beauty of this future with more tenderness and insight, more sympathy and understanding than Hosea, the prophet whose name, like Joshua and Jesus, means Salvation.

Hosea had had a very tragic personal history. His wife, whom he loved with great devotion, had been unfaithful to him, but his love for her was so great that he disregarded the pain and suffering she had caused him and forgave her and took her back in love to his home. Pain and suffering, if rightly understood, teach some of the greatest lessons of life, and out of this experience Hosea learnt great truths which he gave to Israel and through Israel to the world. He saw his own story as an allegory of the story of Israel and Jehovah. Israel had forsaken Jehovah, and in forsaking Him had brought Him pain and grief, but Jehovah loved her and would not let her go. "How shall I give thee up, Ephraim? How shall I deliver thee, Israel? My heart is turned within me, my compassions are kindled together. For I am God and not man; the Holy One in the midst of thee."

Like Amos, Hosea had to teach the people that outward forms and ceremonies were not enough, that true repentance was something deeper than an easy confession and the belief that the offering of sacrifices would bring forgiveness. In the thought of Hosea, Jehovah speaks:

> I will go and return to my place,
> Till they acknowledge their offence, and seek my face:
> In their affliction they will seek me early.

And the people, knowing that they have estranged themselves from Jehovah, say:

Come, and let us return unto the Lord:
For he hath torn, and he will heal us;
He hath smitten, and he will bind us up.
After two days will he revive us:
On the third day he will raise us up,
And we shall live in his sight.
And let us know, let us follow on to know the Lord;
His going forth is sure as the morning:
And he shall come unto us as the rain,
As the latter rain that watereth the earth.[1]

But to such shallow and unreal expressions of penitence, Jehovah replies:

O Ephraim, what shall I do unto thee?
O Judah, what shall I do unto thee?
For your goodness is as a morning cloud,
And as the dew that goeth early away.

. . . .

For I desire mercy, and not sacrifice;
And the knowledge of God more than burnt offerings.[2]

And then, in one great passage after another, Hosea pictures Jehovah pleading with His people, until at length through the infinite strength and tenderness of His Love, Israel turns to Him in true repentance. But before complete restoration can come, Israel must experience the discipline of suffering which would purify her, but beyond that lay a future on which the benediction of Jehovah rested, because His people had turned to Him in

[1]Hosea vi, 1–3, R. V. [2]Hosea vi, 4, 6, R. V.

true repentance and through forgiveness had found the joy that comes from living in communion with Him.

The Fall of Samaria

Jehu was succeeded by his son, a weak king, under whom Israel practically became a vassal of the king of Syria. His successor began to retrieve the fallen fortunes of Israel and under the next king, Jeroboam II, there was a period of success and material prosperity. But after his death there followed a time of unrest. Six kings reigned, four of whom were murdered, and the country easily fell a prey before the Assyrian armies which began to invade Palestine. The last king of Israel was Hoshea, who was attacked and overcome by the king of Assyria and thrown into prison. Israel was forced to pay tribute to Assyria, an Assyrian army surrounded Samaria and besieged it for three years. During these three years a new king, Sargon, came to the throne of Assyria. He was strong and able and completed the conquest which his predecessor had begun. In 722 B.C. Samaria fell, and Northern Israel was made part of the Assyrian Empire. Sargon says of this conquest: "In the beginning of my reign and in the first year of my rule . . . I besieged Samaria and conquered it. Twenty-seven thousand, two hundred and ninety of its inhabitants I carried into captivity; fifty of their chariots I carried away from there to add to my royal fighting force. . . . I restored it again and gave it more population than formerly. I settled their people from the lands I had conquered. I appointed my officers as governors over them. Tribute and customs like those of the Assyrians I imposed upon them."

These new inhabitants of the land were the people known in later Jewish history as the Samaritans. Other conquerors besides the Assyrians were in time to sweep over Palestine, but whereas in the south the people of Judah always resisted stubbornly to the end, the Samaritans seem to have been willing to compromise and to submit to their conquerors. The result has been that they survived, and some of their descendants are still found living in Palestine.

The people of Northern Israel had failed to heed thc tcaching and the appeals of Amos and Hosea, and as both had predicted, the kingdom had fallen. But Judah was still alive and belief in Jehovah, the priceless heritage of the people of Israel, was as yet safe in her hands.

CHAPTER XIV

THE KINGDOM OF JUDAH

Kings of the House of David

WHEN the northern tribes rebelled and established the kingdom of Israel, Rehoboam was left as king of Judah, with Jerusalem as his capital. The kingdom of Judah was never as prosperous as that of Israel. It was a more hilly land and not so easily accessible, the inhabitants were shepherds rather than traders and Jerusalem was the only large town. But the kings of Judah were all descended from David, Jerusalem was the city founded by David and in which was the great temple of Jehovah, the only place where sacrifices might be offered.

The times were warlike and there was little peace in the land. Both Israel and Judah lay between the great empires of the ancient world. Torn with civil strife and constantly at war with each other, they were an easy prey for Egypt on the one hand and Assyria on the other. Yet from the days of the first king, Israel maintained her independence for nearly three hundred years, and Judah for over four hundred.

Rehoboam was succeeded by his son, who reigned for only three years and then Asa became king. We are told that Asa did "that which was right in the eyes of the Lord, as did David his father," and he made a great effort to stamp out idolatry. During his reign there was war between Judah and the northern kingdom, during which Baasha, king of Israel, fortified Ramah, a town a few miles north of Jerusalem. Asa then made friends with Ben-hadad, king of Syria, hoping that he would help in the defeat of Israel by an attack in the rear. Ben-hadad agreed to help and he forced Baasha to stop the fortifying of Ramah.

Asa was in turn succeeded by Jehoshaphat. He followed his father's example in the efforts he made to do that which was right in the sight of the Lord, but like so many of the kings that were to come after him, though he worshipped Jehovah aright himself, he did not do anything to root out the heathen practices that many of the people had adopted.

At this time Ahab was king of Israel.[1] As has been seen Jehoshaphat made peace with him, and his son married Athaliah, the daughter of Ahab and Jezebel. Jehoshaphat reversed the policy of Asa and joined the king of Israel against the Syrians, fighting with Israel in the battle in which Ahab was killed. Jehoshaphat made Jehoram his heir, and when he became king the influence of the daughter of Jezebel was soon felt in the kingdom. He sought to strengthen his position by putting to death all those who in any way opposed him, but he was a weak king. During his reign Judah lost some of her allies, and the Philistines made raids into the country, carrying off prisoners and plunder.

[1]See p. 104 ff.

Jehoram was succeeded by Ahaziah, but he reigned only a year. He was friendly with the king of Israel and was in Samaria when Jehu conspired against the house of Ahab. Ahaziah was caught there by Jehu and slain because he belonged through his mother to the family of Ahab and Jezebel. The death of the king gave his mother the opportunity she wanted to reign herself and introduce Baal worship into Judah. In order to have no rivals, she gave orders that every one who might possibly claim the throne should be killed, and then she reigned herself for six years. But Joash, the one-year-old child of Ahaziah, was hidden by his aunt, and so escaped in the general massacre. During the six years of Athaliah's reign he was brought up by Jehoiada, the high priest. At the end of these years Jehoiada headed a revolution against the queen, in which he was successful. Athaliah was driven out of the palace and slain, and Joash was proclaimed king.

Joash was only seven years old when he became king, and during his minority the kingdom was ruled by Jehoiada. As long as the priest lived, Joash listened to his counsel and the kingdom was well ruled. The chief event of the early part of his reign was the repairing of the temple, which had suffered during the disorders of the previous years. But after the death of Jehoiada the king became careless. War broke out with the king of Syria, who invaded the land and nearly took Jerusalem, but Joash bought him off. Perhaps because of this policy, or it may have been for some other reasons,

Joash became very unpopular. A conspiracy was formed against him and he was murdered.

Three kings then succeeded, under one of whom Judah was fairly prosperous and was able to hold her own against her immediate neighbours who were making war on her borders. Then Ahaz came to the throne. When he became king, the eastern world was gradually being overpowered by Assyria. The kingdom of Israel had already been partially overcome, and the independence of Judah was threatened. It was almost a forlorn hope that the small states in Palestine should be able to withstand the might of Assyria, but Israel and Syria made an alliance and wanted Ahaz to join them. He refused and was threatened with invasion. There were now several courses open to Ahaz. He could join the alliance of Israel and Syria, but if he did so, he would expose himself to the full hostility of Assyria; he could join Assyria and shelter himself under that power against the fury of Israel and Syria; he could make an alliance with Egypt; or he could do nothing and wait and see what the future held in store and shape his policy accordingly.

It was at this crisis that Isaiah, the great Hebrew prophet, went to Ahaz, and in the name of Jehovah besought him to enter no alliance with foreign powers, but to keep to the ancient policy of Judah and trust in Jehovah. But Ahaz would not listen, and he approached Assyria with offers of friendship. Messengers were sent to Tiglath-Pileser, king of Assyria, bearing silver and gold from the temple as gifts and asking for aid against Syria. And then

Ahaz, in his fear, offered sacrifices to the gods of his enemies, in the hope of appeasing them and gaining their help. But the only result of this policy was that foreign gods were introduced into Judah and that the country came into the power of Assyria.

Ahaz was followed by his son Hezekiah. The first act of the new king was to restore the worship of Jehovah. He then had to face an Assyrian invasion. Sennacherib, king of Assyria, invaded Judah, burnt the fields, captured several small towns and would doubtless have besieged Jerusalem, if Hezekiah had not bought him off by sending him tribute of gold. He was obliged to strip the temple of much of its ornament in order to do this, but it saved Jerusalem. It was only for a time, however, for soon after Sennacherib came again, and this time he besieged Jerusalem. But the Assyrians did not remain long in the land, and they left the country without continuing the war. The Hebrew historian tells us that "the angel of the Lord smote them," and an account of the withdrawal of the Assyrian army from before Jerusalem is also given us by the Greek historian Herodotus. He tells us "that there came in the night a multitude of field mice, which devoured all the quivers and bowstrings of the enemy and all the thongs by which they managed their shields. Next morning they commenced their flight and great multitudes fell, as they had no arms to defend themselves." According to a Babylonian record, Sennacherib withdrew from Jerusalem because his army was attacked by a pestilence. That may be the meaning of the story related by Herodotus, for the mouse was an ancient eastern symbol of pestilence.

This deliverance from Sennacherib left a deep mark on the character of the Hebrew people. They saw in it a direct proof of the care of Jehovah for His chosen people and for Jerusalem, the city He had chosen as His sanctuary, the place in which He specially delighted to be worshipped. At this time the belief was gaining ground that Jehovah was not only the God of Israel, but of the whole world and that the mission which lay before Israel was to bring the whole world to acknowledge Jehovah and to worship Him in His holy Temple in Jerusalem. Expression was given to these beliefs in poetry.

God is our hope and strength,
  A very present help in trouble.
Therefore will we not fear, though the earth be moved,
  And though the hills be carried into the midst of the sea;
Though the waters thereof rage and swell,
  And though the mountains shake at the tempest of the same.
    THE LORD OF HOSTS IS WITH US;
    THE GOD OF JACOB IS OUR REFUGE.

The rivers of the flood thereof shall make glad the city of God,
  The holy place of the tabernacle of the most Highest.
God is in the midst of her; therefore shall she not be removed:
  God shall help her, and that right early.
The heathen make much ado, and the kingdoms are moved:
  But God hath showed his voice, and the earth shall melt away.
    THE LORD OF HOSTS IS WITH US;
    THE GOD OF JACOB IS OUR REFUGE.

O come hither, and behold the works of the Lord,
  What destruction he hath brought upon the earth.
He maketh wars to cease in all the world;
  He breaketh the bow, and knappeth the spear in sunder;
  He burneth the chariots in the fire.
Be still, then, and know that I am God:
  I will be exalted among the heathen,
  I will be exalted in the earth.
    The Lord of Hosts is with us;
    The God of Jacob is our refuge.[1]

Hezekiah was a good and able king and under him Judah had a brief span of prosperity. When he died he was buried "in the chiefest of the sepulchres of the sons of David: and all Judah and the inhabitants of Jerusalem did him honour."

Isaiah, the Statesman-Prophet

The greatest of the Hebrew prophets was Isaiah, who lived not long after Amos. Little is known of his life, but his teaching has been kept for us in the great book which bears his name, though he did not write the latter part of it. It is probable that Isaiah belonged to a wealthy and distinguished family, for he seems to have been on terms of intimacy with the priests and rulers of Judah. His writings show that he had been well educated; he knew the history of his nation, and was well versed in foreign affairs; he had a clear, well-trained mind, the understanding of a statesman, and the zeal of a reformer. Isaiah had, too, the imagination of a poet, he had the passionate love of a patriot for his country and above all, he had the inspiration that

[1]Psalm xlvi.

comes from the vision of God. He tells us himself of his call to be a prophet, how one day when he was in the Temple it was suddenly filled for him with the glory of God, and he heard the seraphim sing the hymn of adoration:

> Holy, Holy, Holy is the Lord of Hosts:
> The whole earth is full of His glory.

In his humility he knew himself to be unworthy of the vision, but one of the seraphim touched his lips with fire from the altar and, inspired by the Spirit of God, when he heard a Voice asking for a messenger, he bowed his head and answered, "Here am I, send me."

For forty years and perhaps even longer, after Isaiah had answered the call of Jehovah to serve Him as prophet, he lived in Jerusalem, preaching and teaching, giving his counsel to king and people. One who has once understood something of the vision of God can never afterwards be satisfied with what is petty or mean, dishonourable or corrupt, disloyal or base. Isaiah was filled with a sense of the majesty and glory, the righteousness and holiness of God, and in all his teaching this vision was ever before him.

It was towards the end of the life of Isaiah that the king of Assyria invaded Judah. The king saw the advancing Assyrian army with terror, and Jerusalem gave way to panic. The inhabitants feasted and revelled, "Let us eat, drink and be merry," they said, "for to-morrow we die." Then it was that Isaiah pleaded with them to leave off this mad riot, and he calmed them and restored some confidence and tranquillity. It was at this time that the king bought off the Assyrian with the gold from the Temple. Sennacherib came again later, but in the meantime the wise counsels of the prophet-statesman had prevailed, and when he returned the Assyrian king found a city prepared to resist him.

Isaiah did not confine his attention to the political affairs of the people, he vigorously attacked the crimes of oppression and injustice which they were committing, and he denounced their luxury and their forgetfulness of Jehovah in such a way that he gained great influence. Jerusalem was the centre of the prophet's life, and in the pages of his book we can read descriptions of the city, how she bore herself in her days of triumph, and how she endured famine and siege, loss and defeat. It is a vivid picture of life at a stirring period in the history of a city. Isaiah became the trusted friend and counsellor of the king, and for forty years he was in closest touch with all that concerned the national life and honour. He was a great patriot, but there was nothing narrow in his patriotism. He knew that Judah must one day be destroyed by a foreign invader, but he believed that a remnant would be saved, and he desired for his race that this remnant might be guided by the highest ideals to take its part in service to the world.

The greatest and noblest of the Hebrews have always seemed to possess to a high degree the power of living for the future. The Hebrew race has suffered as few other races have suffered, but even in times of the greatest national suffering and humiliation, the Hebrews have looked forward to a Deliverer who would establish in the world a reign of righteousness and peace. At first the conception of this Deliverer or Messiah was a material one. He was to be a great earthly Conqueror who would set up a kingdom of this world. But to some the longing became greater for one who would renew in Israel the life of the spirit, and in some of the noblest passages of the Old Testament Isaiah gives expression to this idea. He was a man who had vision, he could see in his imagination what lay beyond the present, he knew what standards of uprightness and honour, of goodness and righteousness people might reach if they would only really want to follow those ideals and would believe that it was possible for them to do so. In that day, he told them:

The people that walked in darkness
Have seen a great light:
They that dwell in the land of the shadow of death,
Upon them hath the light shined.

For unto us a child is born,
Unto us a son is given;
And the government shall be upon his shoulder;
And his name shall be called, WONDERFUL, COUNSELLOR,
The MIGHTY GOD, The EVERLASTING FATHER,
The PRINCE OF PEACE.

Of the increase of his government,
And of peace there shall be no end,
Upon the throne of David, and upon his kingdom,

To order it, and to establish it with judgment
And with justice, from henceforth even for ever.[1]

And then Isaiah, the man who had once caught a glimpse of the glory of God, goes on to describe in magnificent language the kingdom of the spirit that should one day be established in the world.

The wilderness and the solitary place shall be glad;
And the desert shall rejoice, and blossom as the rose.
    It shall blossom abundantly,
    And rejoice even with joy and singing;
The glory of Lebanon shall be given unto it,
    The excellency of Carmel and Sharon:
They shall see the glory of the Lord,
    The excellency of our God.

    Strengthen ye the weak hands,
    And confirm the feeble knees.
Say to them that are of a fearful heart,
    Be strong, fear not:
Behold your God will come with vengeance,
    With the recompense of God;
    He will come and save you.

Then the eyes of the blind shall be opened,
And the ears of the deaf shall be unstopped.
Then shall the lame man leap as an hart,
And the tongue of the dumb shall sing:
For in the wilderness shall waters break out,
    And streams in the desert.
And the glowing sand shall become a pool,
And the thirsty ground springs of water:
In the habitation of jackals, where they lay,
Shall be grass with reeds and rushes.

And an highway shall be there,
And a way, and it shall be called The way of holiness;
The unclean shall not pass over it;

[1]Isaiah ix, 2, 6–7.

But it shall be for those:
The wayfaring men, yea fools, shall not err therein.
No lion shall be there,
Nor shall any ravenous beast go up thereon,
They shall not be found there;
But the redeemed shall walk there:
And the ransomed of the Lord shall return,
And come with singing unto Zion;
And everlasting joy shall be upon their heads:
They shall obtain gladness and joy,
And sorrow and sighing shall flee away.[1]

In the thought of Isaiah this kingdom would come when the long-expected Messiah had himself come to reign.

And there shall come forth a rod out of the stem of Jesse,
And a Branch shall grow out of his roots.
And the Spirit of the Lord shall rest upon him,
The spirit of wisdom and understanding,
The spirit of counsel and might,
The spirit of knowledge and of the fear of the Lord;
And shall make him of quick understanding in the fear of the Lord:
And he shall not judge after the sight of his eyes,
Neither reprove after the hearing of his ears;
But with righteousness shall he judge the poor,
And reprove with equity for the meek of the earth:
And he shall smite the earth with the rod of his mouth,
And with the breath of his lips shall he slay the wicked.
And righteousness shall be the girdle of his loins,
And faithfulness the girdle of his reins.

The wolf also shall dwell with the lamb,
And the leopard shall lie down with the kid;
And the calf and the young lion and the fatling together;
And a little child shall lead them.
And the cow and the bear shall feed;

[1]Isaiah xxxv, R. V.

Their young ones shall lie down together:
And the lion shall eat straw like the ox.
And the sucking child shall play on the hole of the asp,
And the weaned child shall put his hand on the cockatrice' den.
They shall not hurt nor destroy
In all my holy mountain:
For the earth shall be full of the knowledge of the Lord,
As the waters cover the sea.[1]

[1] Isaiah xi, 1–9.

CHAPTER XV

THE FALL OF JUDAH

The Reformation Under Josiah

After the death of Hezekiah the history of Judah became the story of a struggle on the part of the nation to keep its national existence. Assyria and Babylon on one side and Egypt on the other were all eager to possess it, and the people were sore beset. Sometimes they would have been willing to make an alliance with the foreign power, but the prophet-statesmen always opposed such a policy, and warned them of what would be the consequences: they would lose their freedom and their national traditions. They also feared the influence of the foreign worship of false gods on the Hebrews. Contact with other nations had already caused the purity of the ancient Hebrew worship to become mixed up with the beliefs of the Egyptians and the Phœnicians, especially with the latter. Commerce had increased and the occupations of the people were changing. There were fewer shepherds and the old hardy simplicity had disappeared. Luxury and soft living had so weakened the character of the people, that a time came when the Syrians were able to send armies without much opposition into the heart of the country, and once Jerusalem was actually sacked by the Egyptians.

On the accession of Manasseh, the son of Hezekiah, a religious reaction set in. Many of the kings of Judah had tolerated idolatry, not so much because they disbelieved in Jehovah, but because their belief in Him as the *only* God was weak, and a toleration of the worship of heathen gods made their policy of forming alliances with foreign nations easier. Manasseh made no effort to restrain the outbreak of heathenism. Not only was heathen worship introduced, but those who refused to bow down to idols were persecuted and the followers of Jehovah were beset with temptations, with anxious cares and fear. Some of the Psalms belong to this period and give voice to their distress.

I cried unto the Lord with my voice;
Yea, even unto the Lord did I make my supplication.
I poured out my complaints before him;
I showed him of my trouble.
  When my spirit was in heaviness,
  Thou knewest my path.

In the way wherein I walked have they privily laid a snare
    for me.
I looked also upon my right hand; and saw there was no
    man that would know me;
I had no place to flee unto;
And no man cared for my soul.
  I cried unto thee, O Lord, and said, Thou art my hope,
  And my portion in the land of the living.

Consider my complaint; for I am brought very low.
O deliver me from my persecutors; for they are too strong
    for me.
Bring my soul out of prison,
That I may give thanks unto thy name;
  Which thing if thou wilt grant me,
  Then shall the righteous resort unto my company.[1]

[1]Psalm cxlii.

This state of affairs lasted through the next reign, and then there came a young king, Josiah, a child when he ascended the throne, but of an eager, zealous personality. As he grew up, the people were becoming conscious of the need for a religious reform. This was chiefly the result of the preaching of the prophet Jeremiah. Influenced by this, when Josiah was eighteen years of age he began by repairing the Temple. Whilst these repairs were in progress, Hilkiah, the High Priest, found in the Temple a copy of the Book of the Law. It was brought to the king and read to him. The denunciations in this book against idolatry were so great that when the king had heard the words of the book, he rent his clothes, and he sent a messenger to Huldah, a prophetess, to ask her advice. She sent back a message that everything would come to pass even as described in the Book of the Law, but that it would not come in the days of Josiah. He should be gathered to his grave in peace, and his eyes would not see the evil that was to befall Jerusalem.

Josiah then set to work to do what he could to effect a reformation. Altars that had been set up to false gods were destroyed; the Temple was prepared once more for a worthy and seemly worship of Jehovah, and the Passover was celebrated with all its ancient dignity.

For a brief period after this reformation, Judah enjoyed a time of peace and prosperity. But it was not to last. The king of Egypt was fighting and conquering in the north of Palestine, and for some reason Josiah decided to go out against him. A battle was fought at Megiddo, in which Josiah was so sorely wounded that he died. He was the last of the good kings of Judah, the last under whom there was any sense of security in the land.

Jeremiah, the Persecuted Prophet

In his desire for reform, Josiah had been influenced by the prophet Jeremiah. Jeremiah was a man of a very different temperament from that of some of the prophets who had preceded him. He was very sensitive; he had neither the energy of Elijah, nor the serene steadfastness of Isaiah. He was often weary and depressed and sick at heart, but in spite of this he never flinched from preaching to the people, facing alike their indifference or hostility. In spite of, or perhaps because of the sensitiveness and delicacy of his spirit which gave him vision and understanding, he went about his work with fearless courage, entreating the people to put their trust in Jehovah and to turn to Him. The result of this preaching was that his life was threatened. At this crisis Jeremiah faced the people calmly and fearlessly, telling them that they might take his life, but that he could not cease preaching what he knew to be true.

The people were impressed by the courage and sincerity of Jeremiah and they spared his life, but he did not stop his preaching. On one occasion he called Baruch, a young scribe, to him and dictated a long appeal to the king and people, warning them of the doom he knew was to descend upon Judah, and bidding them turn to Jehovah and give to Him their ancient loyalty and service. This appeal was read by Baruch to an assembly of the people who had come to the Temple to observe a fast. The news of it was carried to the king, who sent for the roll on which the appeal was written and ordered it to be read to him. It was winter-time and a fire was burning on the hearth in the great hall where the king sat. As he heard the words of warning and of denunciation that were read to him, he seized the roll, cut it in pieces and threw it into the fire where it blazed up and was then burnt to ashes. But Jeremiah had his warnings written down again so that they might be preserved.

The days when Judah would still be free and independent were drawing to a close. The king of Babylon had already made several raids into Palestine, and the kings of Judah were in his power. In their distress, they turned to Egypt, hoping that the king of Egypt would come to their aid and help them against Babylon. He sent an army to Jerusalem and forced the Babylonians to withdraw. As they were departing, Jeremiah left the city and it was thought that this meant that he was about to desert Jerusalem and go over to the enemy. He was seized, brought back to the city and thrown into prison. But imprisonment did not satisfy the chief men of the city, who were angry with Jeremiah because he insisted that destruction was coming upon Jerusalem, and because they feared that such teaching would make the people faint-hearted. So they went to the king and demanded that Jeremiah should be put to death on the grounds that he was disloyal. This time the prophet was thrown down into a dungeon where there was no water, but thick mud.

There were some, however, who were on the side of Jeremiah, and these friends of his rescued him from the dungeon. They were not able to free him, but his imprisonment was made lighter and more bearable. He remained in prison until the fall of Jerusalem.

Jeremiah had foretold ruin and destruction and it came to pass even as he had said. When Jerusalem was taken by the king of Babylon, some of the Hebrews whom he took as captives were sent to Egypt, and Jeremiah went with them. It is not certain how or when he died, but a Hebrew tradition handed down the tale that he was killed by his own countrymen in Egypt.

Jeremiah was a patriot and told the people always what he knew was inevitable, even though it meant the ruin of the city of his people. But in all his teaching there is the confident belief that the immediate desolation that was coming would, if taken and understood rightly, open the way to a more spiritual conception of Jehovah. Above all things he believed that true religion consisted in *knowing* God.

Thus saith the Lord, Let not the wise man glory in his wisdom, neither let the mighty man glory in his might, let not the rich man glory in his riches: but let him that glorieth glory in this, that he understandeth, and knoweth me, that I am the Lord which exercise loving kindness, judgment, and righteousness in the earth: for in these things I delight,

Saith the Lord.[1]

This shall be the covenant that I will make with the house of Israel; After those days, saith the Lord,
I will put my law in their inward parts,
And write it in their hearts;
And I will be their God,
And they shall be my people:
And they shall teach no more every man his neighbour,
And every man his brother,
Saying, Know the Lord:
For they shall all know me,
From the least of them unto the greatest of them,
Saith the Lord:
For I will forgive their iniquity,
And I will remember their sin no more.[2]

Few nations have loved their country with a fiercer or more intense love than the Hebrews, and their patriotism was closely bound up with their religion. Jeremiah lived at a time of great humiliation for his country. These experiences, however, taught him yet another conception of Jehovah which he gave to his people. Jerusalem and the Temple had been destroyed, but Jehovah did not depend for worship on temples made with hands. Out of the suffering and humiliation which came from the exile of his people, Jeremiah learned that as Jehovah was a Spirit, so every soul of man might be His temple, where He could be worshipped in spirit and in truth.

[1]Jeremiah ix, 23–24. [2]Jeremiah xxxi, 33–34.

The Fall of Jerusalem

The reign of Josiah had been the last brief period of prosperity in the history of Judah. Four kings reigned during the twenty years after his death, and they were years of steadily increasing disaster. The power of Babylon was growing stronger, and becoming more and more of a menace to the little kingdom of Judah. At last in 586 B.C. Nebuchadnezzar, king of Babylon, invaded the land. He besieged Jerusalem, captured it, burnt the city, the palaces and the Temple, broke down the walls, carried off what was left of the gold and silver treasures from the Temple and the king's palace, and took nearly all the people as captives to Babylon.

CHAPTER XVI

IN CAPTIVITY

JERUSALEM had been destroyed by Nebuchadnezzar in 586 B.C. and the Hebrews were carried off as captives, chiefly to Babylon, though some were sent to Egypt. Such deporting of whole populations was the usual fate of peoples conquered by the great kings of Assyria and Babylon. For the people of the Hebrew race this was another turning point in their history. Many of the captives never returned to Palestine, those who did were never again completely independent. The final destruction of Jerusalem as a Hebrew city did not take place for six hundred years, but the Captivity of 586 B.C. was the beginning of that long exile which scattered the Hebrew race to every corner of the earth. They went out into a pagan world and were greatly influenced and changed by it, but as a race, they never lost the priceless heritage they had for the world—their faith in Jehovah and the passionate belief that one day deliverance would come. That faith bound them in spirit so closely together that in all the changes of the ages they have remained a distinctive people.

The captivity in Babylon was at first a sad and sorrowful time for the Hebrews. They constantly thought of their own land laid waste by the enemy,

CHART II

B. C.	EGYPT	MESOPOTAMIA, SYRIA and PERSIA	HEBREWS			GREECE	ROME	OTHER PARTS of the WORLD
			Judah	Israel				
9th Century		BENHADAD, King of Syria		AHAB JEHU	ELIJAH ELISHA	LYCURGUS?		
8th Century		ZOROASTER? (Date unknown, perhaps later) SARGON II SENNACHERIB	UZZIAH HEZEKIAH	JEROBOAM II 722 Fall of Samaria	AMOS HOSEA ISAIAH	776 First Olympic Games	753 Rome founded	
7th Century	NECHO defeats JOSIAH at Battle of Megiddo	ASSURBANIPAL  606 Fall of Nineveh	JOSIAH Book of the law discovered			DRACO	Kings in	Phoenicians probably sailed round Africa 
6th Century	525 Egypt a Persian Province P e r s i a	NEBUCHADNEZZAR BELSHAZZAR CYRUS, King of Persia 538 Fall of Babylon n E m DARIUS, King of Persia	586 Fall of Jerusalem Captivity Palestine under Persia 537 First Return under Cyrus Rebuilding of the Temple p i r e		JEREMIAH SECOND ISAIAH DANIEL	SOLON PEISISTRATUS the Tyrant CLEISTHENES THALES of Miletus	Rome  TARQUIN the Proud 509 Roman Republic	BUDDHA in India  CROESUS, King of Lydia CONFUCIUS in China 

and in one of the Psalms written at this time they lament their unhappy fate:

> By the waters of Babylon
> We sat down and wept;
> When we remembered thee, O Zion.
> As for our harps, we hanged them up,
> Upon the trees that are therein.
>
> For they that led us captive required of us then a song,
> And melody in our heaviness;
> Sing us one of the songs of Zion.
> How shall we sing the Lord's song,
> In a strange land?[1]

On the whole the Hebrews do not seem to have been badly treated in Babylon. They "built houses and planted gardens," and life was bearable. The land was described by a Hebrew writer of the time as a "land of traffic, a city of merchants, a fruitful soil, and beside many waters." As long as they paid the tax demanded by the king, and kept the law, they were allowed to rule their own community, and were like a little Hebrew kingdom in the midst of Babylon. Some of the captives even rose to high positions in the kingdom.

The Hebrews learned a great deal from the Babylonians, especially in the way of trading methods, and banking, and they gradually gave up their old agricultural pursuits. They also learned the importance of keeping better written records. Both in Egypt and in Babylon they saw how records were kept everywhere, on the temple walls and on obelisks, on clay tablets and on papyrus rolls. From

[1]Psalm cxxxvii, 1–4.

this time onwards they began to be much more systematic in the way they kept their own records and they began to put into writing the Hebrew tradition as it had come down to them in two ancient documents. These writings became the Hebrew Scriptures and are a part of what we know as the Old Testament.

As a rule, the Hebrews in Babylon were not let or hindered in their worship of Jehovah. Sometimes, however, their refusal to worship any god but the One God brought them into difficulties. Stories were told in later times of the marvels that had befallen those who, in spite of temptation, had remained staunchly true to Jehovah. We are told of the three young men whom Nebuchadnezzar cast into a burning, fiery furnace, because they refused to bow down in worship before the golden image of the king, and of how the fire did them no harm; and of Daniel, who by his ability had risen to an important position and was trusted by the king, but who faced being thrown into a den of lions rather than cease praying to Jehovah, and of how the lions did not touch him.

But in spite of everything the Hebrews were captives, the Temple was in ruins and no sacrifices could be offered in a foreign land, yet they did not lose their belief that they would return. Though a large number of the Psalms written during the Exile show the bitterness of spirit that the national humiliation had wrought in many of the Hebrews, in other Psalms, mingled with the expression of pain, is the joy that will come when the hill of Jerusalem rises up before the returning exile and Jehovah can once more be worshipped in His ancient sanctuary.

Give sentence with me, O God, and defend my cause
against the ungodly people;
O deliver me from the deceitful and wicked man.
For thou art the God of my strength, why hast thou put
me from thee?
And why go I so heavily, while the enemy oppresseth
me?
O send out thy light and thy truth,
That they may lead me;
And bring me unto thy holy hill,
And to thy dwelling.
And that I may go unto the altar of God,
Even unto the God of my joy and gladness;
And upon the harp will I give thanks unto thee,
O God my God.

WHY ART THOU SO HEAVY, O MY SOUL?
AND WHY ART THOU DISQUIETED WITHIN ME?
O PUT THY TRUST IN GOD;
FOR I WILL YET GIVE HIM THANKS,
WHICH IS THE HELP OF MY COUNTENANCE,
AND MY GOD.[1]

On that happy journey back to Jerusalem Jehovah will protect those who put their trust in Him, and some of the exiles, lifted in spirit above the humiliation and suffering of the present put that trust into song.

I will lift up mine eyes unto the hills:
From whence cometh my help.
My help cometh even from the Lord;
Who hath made heaven and earth.

[1]Psalm xliii.

He will not suffer thy foot to be moved:
And he that keepeth thee will not sleep.
Behold, he that keepeth Israel;
Shall neither slumber nor sleep.

The Lord himself is thy keeper;
The Lord is thy defence upon thy right hand.
So that the sun shall not burn thee by day;
Neither the moon by night.

The Lord shall preserve thee from all evil;
Yea, it is even he that shall keep thy soul.
The Lord shall preserve thy going out, and thy coming in;
From this time forth for evermore.[1]

Not quite fifty years after the Captivity, tales were brought to Babylon of Cyrus, the heroic young king of Persia, who had conquered the Medes and was now advancing with his army towards the west. At this time Babylon was ruled by a weak king, and it hardly seemed likely that he would be able to withstand an attack from a general as able as Cyrus. The fate of Babylon was of great importance to the Hebrews, for her conqueror would also be theirs. The years of captivity had taught them many things, but they had also given them great bitterness of spirit, and so they eagerly watched the oncoming of Cyrus as of one who would humiliate Babylon. In 538 B.C. Cyrus reached Babylon. Belshazzar was the king, and on the night of the approach of Cyrus he was giving a great feast to the nobles of the land. At this feast the gold and silver vessels which Nebuchadnezzar had taken from Jerusalem were brought out and

[1]Psalm cxxi.

the Babylonians drank wine from them. In the midst of the feast, a strange hand appeared and wrote some mysterious words on the wall opposite the king. None of his wise men could interpret the words, but it was known that the young Hebrew Daniel was gifted in such matters, and they sent for him. He told the king that the words meant that he had been tried and weighed in the balance and found wanting, that his days were numbered, and that his kingdom should be given to the Persians.

This feast was probably the last revel before the attack of the Persians and the defeat of the Babylonians. In that night Belshazzar was slain and the Persian became lord of the land.

CHAPTER XVII

THE RETURN FROM EXILE

The Rebuilding of Jerusalem

CYRUS, king of Persia, was one of the great hero-figures of the ancient world. The men of that world were always more ready to be influenced by a great leader than by an idea. Cyrus was just such a leader, and in his ideals he stands far above most of the other rulers of his time. He was both a good general and a wise statesman. He did not try to force those whom he had conquered to obey him by crushing and oppressing them, he endeavoured to secure their loyalty by acts of kindness and a policy of generosity. Wherever it was possible, he allowed native princes to rule over the different parts of his empire, and in one of his inscriptions he says: "The gods whose sanctuaries from of old had lain in ruins I brought back again to their dwelling-places and caused them to reside there for ever. All the citizens of those lands I assembled and I restored them to their homes." The Hebrews shared in this generous and far-seeing policy and a large number of the exiles were allowed to return to Jerusalem.

The first thing they set about doing was to rebuild the Temple. But the rebuilding did not continue under peaceful conditions. They made enemies. Certain Samaritans who were living in Palestine offered their services to aid in this rebuilding. The Hebrews regarded these Samaritans as men who had failed to keep the ancient worship of Jehovah in its purity and they refused the offer of help. This refusal was not only an ungracious act towards those who were willing to be friendly as neighbours, but it was the beginning of that policy of exclusiveness and of emphasis on formalism which was to be such a snare to them later.

Angry at this rebuff, the Samaritans sent a letter to the king of Persia telling him that Judah had always been a turbulent state and requesting that measures be taken to stop the rebuilding of Jerusalem. The result of this interference was that the work was stopped for a time, but later, however, an appeal to the king of Persia from the Hebrews for permission to go on with the rebuilding was heard and granted.

The work was begun again at once, and in 516 B.C., seventy years after its destruction by Nebuchadnezzar, the Temple was completed. We are told that the "children of Israel, the priests and the Levites, and the rest of the children of the captivity, kept the dedication of this house of God with joy," and their joy found expression in noble hymns of praise:

O sing unto the Lord a new song:
For He hath done marvellous things.
With His own right hand, and with His holy arm:
Hath He gotten Himself the victory.
The Lord declared His salvation:
His righteousness hath He openly showed in the sight of the heathen.

He hath remembered His mercy and truth toward the house of Israel:
And all the ends of the world have seen the salvation of our God.
Show yourselves joyful unto the Lord, all ye lands:
Sing, rejoice, and give thanks.

Praise the Lord upon the harp:
Sing to the harp with a psalm of thanksgiving.
With trumpets also, and shawms:
O show yourselves joyful before the Lord the King.
Let the sea make a noise, and all that therein is:
The round world, and they that dwell therein.
Let the floods clap their hands, and let the hills be joyful together before the Lord:
For He is come to judge the earth.
With righteousness shall He judge the world:
And the people with equity.[1]

And again:

O be joyful in the Lord, all ye lands.
Serve the Lord with gladness,
And come before his presence with a song.

Be ye sure that the Lord he is God;
It is he that hath made us, and not we ourselves;
We are his people and the sheep of his pasture.

O go your way into his gates with thanksgiving,
And into his courts with praise;
Be thankful unto him, and speak good of his name.

For the Lord is gracious;
His mercy is everlasting;
And his truth endureth from generation to generation.[2]

About seventy years after the rebuilding of the Temple, there were still Hebrews in the service of

[1]Psalm xcviii. [2]Psalm c.

the Persian king living far away from Jerusalem in the Persian capital. One of these was Nehemiah, and a group of his fellow-countrymen from Jerusalem came to him and told him of the bad conditions of the city of Jerusalem. The Temple had been rebuilt, but the walls of the city were broken down and the inhabitants in great distress.

Nehemiah was the chief cup-bearer of the king of Persia. He took a favourable opportunity to plead the cause of Jerusalem and to beg for permission to return with those of his fellow-countrymen who wished and to rebuild the walls. The permission was granted and Nehemiah superintended the work. He had many difficulties to contend with, but in the end the walls were built and Jerusalem restored to something of its old dignity and security.

The rebuilding of the Temple and of the walls of Jerusalem was of great importance to the Hebrews. They were not an independent kingdom, yet they had once more a common meeting-place in their ancient sanctuary. The Hebrews never regained complete political independence, but from this time onward they were all members of the Jewish Church, and they were now called Jews more often than Hebrews. In the centuries following their return to Jerusalem they completed their history, they wrote down their law, and they recorded their great religious experiences. They were always hoping for a political deliverer who would free them from foreign rule. In reality they were unconsciously preparing the way for a spiritual deliverer who would set them free from bondage to the letter of the law, whose kingdom of the spirit would include all men of all the nations of the earth, and whose rule would be that of Righteousness and Peace. Some of the finest of the Jews realised something of this already and gave expression to it in their poetry:

God be merciful unto us, and bless us,
And show us the light of his countenance, and be merciful unto us;
That thy way may be known upon earth,
Thy saving health among all nations.
LET THE PEOPLE PRAISE THEE, O GOD;
YEA, LET ALL THE PEOPLE PRAISE THEE.

O let the nations rejoice
And be glad;
For thou shalt judge the folk righteously
And govern the nations upon earth.
LET THE PEOPLE PRAISE THEE, O GOD;
YEA, LET ALL THE PEOPLE PRAISE THEE.

Then shall the earth bring forth her increase;
And God, even our own God, shall give us his blessing.
God shall bless us;
And all the ends of the world shall fear him.
LET THE PEOPLE PRAISE THEE, O GOD;
YEA, LET ALL THE PEOPLE PRAISE THEE.[1]

The Unknown Prophet

At some time, probably towards the end of the Captivity, one of the last of the great Hebrew prophets arose. He is sometimes known as Second Isaiah, because his writings form the second part

[1]Psalm lxvii.

of the book called by the name of Isaiah. Nothing is known of him, and it is not certain where he lived, but his words have been kept for us, and he was one of the last of the prophets who pointed the way to a great ideal.

The Jews were often discouraged at the difficulties that beset them. Second Isaiah was convinced that deliverance was coming to the people of Jehovah, but running through all that he said was the conviction that it was deliverance not only from the foreign oppressor that Israel needed, but much more from the bondage of sin. He believed that a great destiny awaited his people and that they had a service to perform for the world, but he believed that that service could only be performed through willing self-sacrifice and suffering for others.

He began by words of comfort for the people and the expectation of coming deliverance.

Comfort ye, comfort ye, my people, saith your God.
Speak ye comfortably to Jerusalem, and cry unto her,
That her warfare is accomplished,
That her iniquity is pardoned:
For she hath received of the Lord's hand double for all her sins.

O Zion, that bringest good tidings,
Get thee up into the high mountain;
O Jerusalem, that bringest good tidings,
Lift up thy voice with strength;
Lift it up, be not afraid;
Say unto the cities of Judah, Behold your God!

Behold the Lord God will come with strong hand,
And his arm shall rule for him:

Behold, his reward is with him,
   And his work before him.
He shall feed his flock like a shepherd,
He shall gather the lambs with his arm,
And carry them in his bosom,
And shall gently lead those that are with young.

Then he went on to give them in great poetry a magnificent conception of Jehovah:

Who hath measured the waters in the hollow of his hand,
   And meted out heaven with the span,
   And comprehended the dust of the earth in a measure,
   And weighed the mountains in scales,
         And the hills in a balance?
Who hath directed the Spirit of the Lord,
Or being his counsellor hath taught him?
With whom took he counsel, and who instructed him,
   And taught him in the path of judgment,
   And taught him knowledge,
   And showed to him the way of understanding?

Have ye not known?
Have ye not heard?
Hath it not been told you from the beginning?
Have ye not understood from the foundations of the earth?

It is he that sitteth upon the circle of the earth,
And the inhabitants thereof are as grasshoppers;
That stretcheth out the heavens as a curtain,
And spreadeth them out as a tent to dwell in:
That bringeth the princes to nothing;
   He maketh the judges of the earth as vanity.

To whom then will ye liken me,
Or shall I be equal,
         Saith the Holy One.
Lift up your eyes on high, and behold
Who hath created these things,

That bringeth out their host by number.
He calleth them all by names;
By the greatness of his might,
For that he is strong in power;
Not one faileth.[1]

Later, this Unknown Prophet describes the character of one who has come to be called the Suffering Servant, one who through the willing offering of himself will serve others.

He is despised and rejected of men;
A man of sorrows, and acquainted with grief:
And we hid as it were our faces from him;
He was despised
And we esteemed him not.

Surely he hath borne our griefs and carried our sorrows:
Yet we did esteem him stricken, smitten of God, and afflicted.
But he was wounded for our transgressions,
He was bruised for our iniquities:
The chastisement of our peace was upon him;
And with his stripes we are healed.
All we like sheep have gone astray;
We have turned everyone to his own way;
And the Lord hath laid on him the iniquity of us all.[2]

The thought of deliverance runs all through the teaching of this prophet. Sometimes he describes the Deliverer.

Behold my servant, whom I uphold;
Mine elect, in whom my soul delighteth;
I have put my spirit upon him;
He shall bring forth judgment to the Gentiles.
He shall not cry, nor lift up, nor cause his voice to be heard in the street.

[1]From Isaiah xl. [2]Isaiah liii, 3–6.

A bruised reed shall he not break,
And the smoking flax shall he not quench:
He shall bring forth judgment unto truth,
He shall not fail nor be discouraged,
Till he have set judgment in the earth:
And the isles shall wait for his law.[1]

The Spirit of the Lord God is upon me;
Because the Lord hath anointed me to preach good tidings unto the meek;
He hath sent me to bind up the brokenhearted,
  To proclaim liberty to the captives,
  And the opening of the prison to them that are bound;
  To proclaim the acceptable year of the Lord,
    And the day of vengeance of our God.
  To comfort all that mourn;
  To appoint unto them that mourn in Zion,
  To give unto them beauty for ashes,
    The oil of joy for mourning,
    The garment of praise for the spirit of heaviness;
That they might be called trees of righteousness,
  The planting of the Lord,
    That he might be glorified.[2]

Sometimes he describes the joy in the land after the appearance of the Deliverer and what will be the character of his rule:

  Sing, O heavens;
  And be joyful, O earth;
  And break forth into singing, O mountains:
For the Lord hath comforted his people,
And will have mercy upon his afflicted.[3]

  For the Lord shall comfort Zion:
  He will comfort all her waste places,
  And he will make her wilderness like Eden
      And her desert like the garden of the Lord;

[1] Isaiah xlii, 1–4.
[2] Isaiah lxi, 1–3.
[3] Isaiah xlix, 13.

Joy and gladness shall be found therein,
Thanksgiving, and the voice of melody.

The redeemed of the Lord shall return,
And come with singing unto Zion;
And everlasting joy shall be upon their head:
They shall obtain gladness and joy;
And sorrow and mourning shall flee away.[1]

For ye shall go out with joy,
And be led forth with peace:
The mountains and the hills shall break forth before you into singing,
And all the trees of the field shall clap their hands.
Instead of the thorn shall come up the fir tree,
And instead of the brier shall come up the myrtle tree:
And it shall be to the Lord for a name,
For an everlasting sign that shall not be cut off.[2]

The vision of Second Isaiah was a wide one, and in his thought he saw the whole world brought into allegiance to Jehovah:

Arise, shine;
For thy light is come,
And the glory of the Lord is risen upon thee.
For, behold, darkness shall cover the earth,
And gross darkness the people:
But the Lord shall arise upon thee,
And his glory shall be seen upon thee.
And nations shall come to thy light,
And kings to the brightness of thy rising.

Lift up thine eyes round about, and see:
They all gather themselves together,
They come to thee:
Thy sons shall come from far,
And thy daughters shall be carried in the arms.
Then thou shalt see, and be lightened,

[1]Isaiah li, 3, 11. [2]Isaiah lv, 12–13.

And thine heart shall tremble, and be enlarged;
Because the abundance of the sea shall be turned unto
thee,
The wealth of the nations shall come unto thee.[1]

But the people were often cast down and discouraged, for to them the day of deliverance seemed far off. Then it was that the Prophet showed them the tenderness of Jehovah, and turned their thoughts to the idea of a deliverance of the spirit, to the attainment of which Jehovah was ready to help them with His love, His tender understanding of their difficulties, and the strengthening comfort of His Presence.

Fear thou not, for I am with thee;
Be not dismayed, for I am thy God:
I will strengthen thee;
Yea, I will help thee;
Yea, I will uphold thee
With the right hand of my righteousness.

For I the Lord thy God will hold thy right hand,
Saying unto thee, Fear not; I will help thee.[2]

Hast thou not known?
Hast thou not heard?
That the everlasting God, the Lord,
The Creator of the ends of the earth,
Fainteth not, neither is weary?
There is no searching of his understanding.
He giveth power to the faint;
And to them that have no might he increaseth
strength.
Even the youths shall faint and be weary,
And the young men shall utterly fall;
But they that wait upon the Lord shall renew their
strength;

[1]Isaiah lx, 1–5, R. V. [2]Isaiah, xli, 10, 13.

They shall mount up with wings as eagles;
They shall run and not be weary;
And they shall walk, and not faint.[1]

Jerusalem Under the High Priests

Years went by, the Temple had been restored, and the walls of Jerusalem rebuilt, but all was not well with the Jewish people. Not all those who had been taken into captivity had returned; the land was still under a foreign ruler; the leaders were not men like Isaiah, who was filled with the spirit that came to one to whom had been given a vision of God, nor like Hosea, tender in his understanding of the love of God, nor like Jeremiah with his insight into the life of the Spirit. The result was a general lowering of standards: the men began to marry heathen wives and the worship of heathen gods became common; those who attended the Temple services became careless in outward reverence, and the perfunctory way in which the priests performed their duties did not bring the people to a realisation of the Unseen God. With the lowering of religious ideals came also a lowering of other ideals: there was class rivalry and oppression of the poor.

Ezra and Nehemiah, honest, able, practical and God-fearing men, tried as leaders of the people to improve this state of affairs by certain reforms. Nehemiah, in particular, attacked social conditions. He forbade marriages with heathen women, he enforced the law concerning the observance of the

[1]Isaiah xl, 28–31.

Sabbath, he insisted on greater strictness in the keeping of religious feasts and more reverence in the performance of the Temple services.

Ezra was a scribe and he had brought the Book of the Law from Babylon and had it read to the people. This Book of the Law had been compiled during the Exile and the Return and was practically the Pentateuch as we know it. The Law emphasised three things. It explained in great detail the function and duties of the High Priest, the Priests and the Levites. At this period the High Priest was becoming more and more not only the religious head of the nation, but its civil ruler as well. The political independence of the Jews was lost and they were governed by a foreign power, which fortunately recognised the importance of the High Priest and a good deal of authority was given him. He was expected to keep order in the state, and to see that the taxes were duly paid, but beyond that he was very independent.

The Book of the Law next prescribed the worship of the Jews. Great importance was attached to the keeping of the Sabbath. This observance was one of the things that distinguished the Jewish from most other ancient religions. The latter did not as a rule, except in Babylonia, require the setting apart of one special day a week for worship. Worship is not confined to one day or one place, but the setting apart of one day, and the meeting together in one place, is of great value and importance. It is an outward symbol of loyalty to God and of fellowship with others.

The chief Jewish feasts were also described. These were the Passover, in memory of the Exodus from Egypt, the Feast of Pentecost, a thanksgiving for the harvest, celebrated fifty days after the Passover, and the Feast of Tabernacles, another thanksgiving for the gathering in of the corn and wine and oil. There was also a day set apart every year called the Day of Atonement, a day of national fasting and humiliation, when the scapegoat was sent out into the wilderness as a symbol that the sins of the people had been put upon him and taken away from them. The Book of the Law also prescribed a year of Jubilee, to be celebrated in every fiftieth year. During this year all agriculture was to stop in order that the soil might lie fallow, all debts were to be forgiven, and slaves were to be set free.

In the third place, the Book of the Law laid great stress on how the Jews were to think of Jehovah, that He was the One and Only God, Almighty and Holy, in order, as the Unknown Prophet of the Exile put it, "that they may know from the rising of the sun, and from the west, that there is none beside me. I am the Lord, and there is none else." Special times and places, the Sabbath and the Temple, and a special people, the Jews, were set apart as belonging in a peculiar way to Him.

The influence of the Law on the Jewish Church at this time was very great. It made the Jewish religion very formal, for the Law provided for so many details, that gradually nothing was accepted

CHART III

B. C.	EGYPT	MESOPOTAMIA, SYRIA and PERSIA	HEBREWS	GREECE	ROME	OTHER PARTS of the WORLD
5th Century		XERXES, King of Persia (Known to the Hebrews as Ahasuerus) 	458 Return to Jerusalem under EZRA NEHEMIAH Rebuilding of the Walls of Jerusalem	Persian Wars Athenian Empire PERICLES Peloponnesian War SOCRATES 401 March of the Ten Thousand	494 Secession of the Plebs to Mons Sacer CORIOLANUS 450 Laws of the Twelve Tables CINCINNATUS	
4th Century	E m Ptolemies in	p i r e o f	Palestine part of Alexander's Empire A l e x a n d e r t h e	PLATO ARISTOTLE G r e a t	Roman Conquest of Italy 	
3rd Century	Egypt		Palestine under Egypt	ARCHIMEDES	War with Pyrrhus Punic Wars HANNIBAL 	
2nd Century		ANTIOCHUS the Great ANTIOCHUS EPIPHANES	Palestine under Syria Jews under the High Priests 167 Revolt under JUDAS MACCABEUS	146 Destruction of Corinth	M. CATO The GRACCHI	146 Destruction of Carthage
1st Century	 CLEOPATRA R o	m a n	63 Palestine conquered by POMPEY E m HEROD the Great	p i r	MARIUS SULLA JULIUS CAESAR  e AUGUSTUS	55 Julius Caesar invaded Britain 
A. D. 1st Century to 70			**BIRTH OF CHRIST**  ST. PAUL 70 Destruction of Jerusalem		TIBERIUS CALIGULA CLAUDIUS NERO VESPASIAN 	43 Roman Conquest of Britain

unless it was found to be written in the Book of the Law. The great Hebrew prophets had gradually turned the people to a conception of religion which was world-wide; the Jews at this period narrowed it to that of a national church that was becoming increasingly intolerant, because of its emphasis on the Law instead of the Spirit.

But there was another side to the Jewish religion at this time. Up and down the country were people described by the Psalmist as those who were "quiet in the land," whose religion is reflected in many of the Psalms written at this time. They were men who, if they were narrow, were yet of deep and steadfast faith in God, and tender in their pity towards the poor and afflicted. All through this period of political confusion and turmoil, there were Jews whose hearts were set on God and who in the darkest days of their history still looked for the Deliverer promised of old.

CHAPTER XVIII

ISRAEL UNDER THE GREEKS AND ROMANS

The Hellenistic Period

The Jews remained under Persian rule until Persia was in its turn conquered by Alexander the Great. At his death, his vast empire was divided up and Judæa was a much-coveted land owing to its favourable position. It was the natural frontier between Syria and Egypt, it was rich in timber, and provided another route to India besides that by way of the Nile and Red Sea. For a hundred years Egypt and Syria strove for possession of Judæa, sometimes one and sometimes the other victorious, but in 198 B.C. the king of Syria gained a decisive victory over Egypt and Judæa passed under his control. It remained part of the dominion of Syria until it was finally taken by the Romans in 63 B.C.

Beginning with Alexander, Greek civilisation had stepped out into a new age. Greece was no longer living for herself, her civilisation had been far flung over Asia. The Barbarian adopted Greek customs and Greece was the teacher of the world in science, in art, and in all that was meant by civilised living. The old Greek idea of the city-state had broken down, and men were thinking now in terms of empire rather than in terms of small individual states. Greek ways of thinking, and the Greek philosophy of life were widely accepted, but in Judæa, Greek culture met an unexpected check.

In a world in which barriers of race and varying cultures were breaking down, the Jew stubbornly remained a Jew and regarded himself as part of the Jewish nation and of none other. Though the Jew had accepted the fact taught by the great prophets that Jehovah was the God of the whole world, he still had to learn the practical results of such a belief. This teaching was put before him at this time in the story of Jonah, the poetical biography of a prophet with a divided loyalty, a prophet who was commissioned by Jehovah to take a divine message to the hated enemy of his people.

Though racially the Jew remained a Jew, distinct from other Mediterranean races, he was, nevertheless, profoundly influenced by Greek civilisation. In this Hellenistic period commerce increased with the outside world. The Jews established colonies of their own in all the great cities of the eastern Mediterranean, particularly in Alexandria. City life increased in Judæa and the cities were filled with great buildings built after Greek models. Hebrew was still the language of the worship and the learning of the Jew, but for ordinary conversation Greek was more and more used. The foundation of Greek civilisation was philosophy, and to the Greek *wisdom* meant the highest achievements possible to the mind of man. The foundation of Hebrew civilisation was religion, and to the Jew *wisdom* meant the *fear of the Lord,* and by *fear* he meant the reverent surrender of oneself to the will of God. The righteousness of the Hebrew was based on no teaching of reward or punishment in an after life, he had no clear notions of either heaven or hell. He believed in doing right because it was the will of God, and this to him was *wisdom*. This Hebrew idea of wisdom is magnificently set forth in the story of Job, the man who had no answer to the question of why suffering and pain are in the world, but who found his own satisfaction in reverent surrender of himself to God.

The questioning mind of the Greek influenced Jewish thought in various ways, but particularly in respect to the question of immortality. Earlier Jewish teaching had been vague on this subject. After this life there was Sheol, but it was a shadowy place about which his beliefs were uncertain and indefinite. But from this period onwards the belief in immortality grew and was expressed more and more definitely. Jewish hopes had always been fixed on a new world when righteousness should reign, and during this period of national humiliation under foreign rulers, the Jews began to think more of another life and to have hopes of happiness after death. It was one of the Jewish thinkers of this period who wrote: "The souls of the righteous are in the hand of God, and there shall no torment touch them. In the sight of the unwise they seemed to die: and their departure is taken for misery, and their going from us to be utter destruction: but they are in peace. For though they be punished in the sight of men, yet is their hope full of immortality. And having been a little chastised, they shall be greatly rewarded: for God proved them, and found them worthy for himself.

As gold in the furnace hath he tried them, and received them as a burnt offering. And in the time of their visitation they shall shine, and run to and fro like sparks among the stubble. They shall judge the nations, and have dominion over the people, and their Lord shall reign for ever. They that put their trust in him shall understand the truth: and such as be faithful in love shall abide with him: for grace and mercy is to his saints, and he hath care for his elect."[1]

A good deal of the Jewish literature of this period consists of what is called the Wisdom Literature. Much of it, as in the book of Proverbs, was practical and sometimes prosaic, it did not inspire the nation with great ideals, but it gave an everyday philosophy of kindliness and commonsense.

Under the influence of Hellenism, schools were established in Judæa. They were generally attached to the synagogues, and the teachers were Jewish scribes. The Scriptures were the foundation of the moral teaching given and these schools were of great importance in training the character of the Jewish child.

The Temple in Jerusalem was too far away for the Jew to go to it oftener than for the greater feasts. The worship there was the outward symbol of the national loyalty to Jehovah; the weekly worship of prayer and praise and scripture-reading belonged to the Synagogue. It was in the synagogues throughout the country-side that the strongest Jewish element was now to be found, and because of

[1]Wisdom of Solomon (Apocrypha), iii, 1–9.

the emphasis placed there on prayer and praise and scripture-reading rather than on sacrifice, the Jewish mind was being unconsciously prepared for the time when the Temple would be finally destroyed and there would no longer be a national centre for the ancient sacrificial worship of Jehovah.

The Maccabees

Towards the middle of the second century B.C. the king of Syria was Antiochus Epiphanes. This king aimed at making his kingdom a completely Hellenised state, and he determined that the Jews should adopt Greek customs and share in the Greek culture of the rest of his dominions. He deposed the High Priest and put in his place a man who was known as having Hellenistic sympathies. There were large numbers of Jews in Jerusalem who had Hellenistic tastes and up to a certain point Antiochus seemed to be succeeding in his aims. But revolts broke out in Judæa, and Antiochus himself went to quell them. The result of this was a period of persecution for the Jews. Antiochus was a despot and cruel, and he was determined to stamp out Jewish resistance. He knew that the strength of the Jews was in their religion, and so he attacked that. The observance of Jewish rites and ceremonies was forbidden on pain of death, and attempts were made to force the Jews to practise heathen rites. The Temple was plundered and a pagan altar erected in it. Search was made for copies of the Books of the Law. When they were found, they were destroyed, and to possess them was a penal offence.

These attacks upon the Temple made the Jews realise that the conflict was not one merely between Jewish and Hellenistic customs and manners, dress or language, but between loyalty to Jehovah or Olympian Zeus. Their opposition became stubborn and determined and they made a vigorous resistance under a heroic leader, Judas Maccabæus. He was a brilliant general and he inspired his army with courage. He had only a small and poorly equipped following, but the men who composed it were patriots and inspired by an intense enthusiasm for their religion. They had against them well-trained soldiers, armed with the best weapons of the time, and amongst them were Jews who had deserted their own side, who knew every inch of the country and who could spy out all their movements. But in spite of these odds, Judas Maccabæus succeeded in gaining victories, until at last he was able to enter Jerusalem.

On the death of Antiochus Epiphanes, the Jews were left free to worship again in the Temple, and Judas Maccabæus restored and rededicated the altar of Jehovah. This festival was known as the Feast of the Dedication, or the Feast of Lights (because one of its customs was the illuminating of all private houses), a festival which is still observed. But peace did not last very long, and when another Syrian army invaded the land, Judas Maccabæus was defeated and killed in battle, and his army fled.

This defeat seemed like a death blow to the Jewish hopes for freedom, but soon after the death of Judas Maccabæus the kingdom of Syria began to grow weaker, and the Jews acquired a certain amount of independence. They made efforts to extend the boundaries of their land and to hasten the time when the desires of the nation for its own freedom and for uniting the world in loyalty and allegiance to Jehovah should come to pass.

The Romans and the Destruction of Jerusalem

In 133 B.C. Syria had become a Roman province. Judæa was nominally under the control of the Pro-Consul of Syria, but she was free to worship as she chose, and she controlled a good part of her domestic affairs. But the Jews could not agree among themselves and ceaseless strife prevailed between the different factions. The result was that in 63 B.C. when Pompey was in the east, he entered Jerusalem, subdued it, took large numbers of Jews as slaves to Rome, and the country passed completely under Roman rule. Rome was not popular with the people, but her strong hand kept peace and she sent governors to maintain her authority. These rulers grew in power until in 39 B.C. Herod, the ruler of the time, was given the title of King.

This Herod, known later as Herod the Great, was a strong-willed, merciless, unscrupulous ruler, but he was shrewd, and knew that to rule the Jews he must appear to be their friend. He kept order, increased the prosperity of the land by great public works, aqueducts, sea-ports, Greek baths, stoa, and new cities. He rebuilt the Temple at Jerusalem, making it larger and more splendid than it had been at any time since the days of Solomon. Samaria was restored and Cæsarea built, the latter becoming the second city of importance in the kingdom. In spite of all his efforts, however, Herod was always disliked by the Jews. He had too many Greek sympathies, he was in reality a tyrant, and in order to stand well with Rome he governed in his own interests, and not really in the interests of the Jews.

The time was fast coming when the Jews were to live in Judæa no longer. After the death of Herod the Great, the Roman rulers grew more tyrannical. The Jews resented the presence of Roman garrisons in their cities, and they were oppressed by heavy taxation. They grew more and more angry at the indignities heaped upon them, until at last open rebellion broke out, and there was war. It reached its height in A.D. 70, when Titus, the son of the Roman Emperor, came against Jerusalem and besieged it. The city was crowded for the Feast of the Passover, and famine and pestilence soon appeared in the city. Titus broke through the outer walls and at last the Jews took refuge in the Temple, which was almost like a fortress. Then a Roman soldier threw a flaming torch into the Temple, and a blazing fire broke out. After that the end soon came; the Temple was burnt and the whole city razed to the ground, except three towers and a part of the wall, which were left in order that the whole world might know how strong was the city taken by Rome. Those of the Jews who had survived, and a few of the vessels from the Temple which had escaped destruction, were taken to be shown as triumphal spoils when Titus returned to Rome.

Never again have the Jews ruled as a nation in Palestine.

Was this the end of the Jewish hopes, of the new and better world that Isaiah had predicted, of the Deliverer whom they expected? The laws of the Jews had become very definite, their religious beliefs very rigid; long years of oppression had given a tinge of melancholy to their thought and had taken the joyousness out of life. The very fact that they were a small and politically unimportant nation made them cling to all their old traditions and customs, and this made them narrow and intolerant.

But, whatever their faults, they had developed an enthusiastic zeal for the things of God's kingdom, and they never wavered in their belief that underneath all history there was a plan. The experiences of their history had taught them that there was only one God, and that belief brings with it the recognition that everything in human life is part of one ordered plan. They had learned what was the character of God, and so they believed that there would come a day when Righteousness would reign throughout the world. They needed an interpreter whose character and teaching would show them, and through them the world, the way to the fulfilment of all that was best and noblest in their hopes.

In the fulness of time, the Teacher came. At Bethlehem, in the days of Herod the King, seventy years before the destruction of Jerusalem, Christ was born, who by His life and teaching made possible the fulfilment of the ancient visions.

I

REFERENCE LIST OF BIBLE STORIES

II

SUGGESTIONS ABOUT BOOKS FOR FURTHER READING

REFERENCE LIST OF BIBLE STORIES

CHAPTER III. EARLY HEBREW TALES

The Creation	Genesis	i, ii, 1–3.
The Garden of Eden	"	ii, 8–17; iii.
Cain and Abel	"	iv, 1–16.
The Flood	"	vi, 9–22; vii, viii, ix, 8–17.
The Tower of Babel	"	xi, 1–9.

CHAPTER IV. THE FOUNDERS OF THE HEBREW NATION

The Call of Abraham	Genesis	xii, 1–9.
Lot's Choice	"	xiii.
Abraham's Rescue of Lot	"	xiv, 10–24.
Abraham Entertains Angels	"	xviii, 1–8.
Sodom and Gomorrah	"	xviii, 17–33; xix, 1–3, 12–29.
Hagar and Ishmael	"	xvi, 7–13; xxi, 9–21.
The Sacrifice of Isaac	"	xxii, 1–19.
Abraham's Purchase of the Cave of Machpelah	"	xxiii.
Rebekah, the Bride of Isaac	"	xxiv.
Jacob and Esau	"	xxv, 27–34; xxvii.
Jacob's Dream	"	xxviii, 10–22.
Jacob and Rachel	"	xxix, 1–20.
Jacob's Return to Esau	"	xxxii, 3–23; xxxiii, 1–17.
Jacob Wrestling with the Angel	"	xxxii, 24–31.
Joseph and His Dreams	"	xxxvii, 3–36.
Joseph in Prison	"	xxxix, 20–23; xl.
The Pharaoh's Dreams	"	xli.
Joseph and His Brothers	"	xlii, xliii, xliv, xlv.
Jacob in Egypt	"	xlvi, 1–7, 28–34; xlvii, 1–12.
Death and Burial of Jacob	"	xlvii, 27–31; xlviii.
Death of Joseph	"	l, 22–26.

CHAPTER V. MOSES AND THE EXODUS FROM EGYPT

Story	Book	Reference
The Hebrews in Egypt	Exodus	i.
The Birth of Moses	"	ii, 1–10.
Flight of Moses	"	ii, 11–22.
Moses at the Burning Bush	"	iii, iv, 1–17.
Moses and the Pharaoh	"	v.
The Ten Plagues	"	vii, viii, ix, x, xi.
The Passover	"	xii, 1–28.
The Exodus	"	xii, 29–42; xiii, 17–22.
The Red Sea	"	xiv.
Thanksgiving Song of Moses	"	xv, 1–22.

CHAPTER VI. THE MAKING OF THE HEBREW NATION

Story	Book	Reference
Food and Water in the Wilderness	Exodus	xvi, xvii, 1–7.
Fighting the Amalekites	"	xvii, 9–16.
Jethro's Counsel to Moses	"	xviii, 5–27.
At Mount Sinai	"	xix, 16–25; xxiv, 12–18.
The Ten Commandments	"	xx, 1–17.
The Golden Calf	"	xxxii, 1–6, 15–24, 30–34.
The Tabernacle	"	xxxi, 1–11; xxxv, 4–35; xl.
The Spies	Numbers	xiii, 1–12, 17–33.
Rebellion of Korah. Dathan and Abiram	"	xvi, 2–35.
Moses Strikes the Rock for Water	"	xx, 1–13.
Edom Refuses Passage to the Hebrews	"	xx, 14–21.
Death of Aaron	"	xx, 22–29.
The Fiery Serpents	"	xxi, 4–9.
Fighting with Sihon and Og	"	xxi, 21–25, 33–35.
Balak and Balaam	"	xxii, xxiii, xxiv, 1–19, 25.
Death of Moses	Deuteronomy	xxxi, 1–8; xxxiv.

CHAPTER VII. THE CONQUEST OF CANAAN AND THE AGE OF THE JUDGES

Story	Book	Reference
The Call of Joshua	Numbers	xxvii, 18–23, and Joshua i.
Spies Sent to Jericho	Joshua	ii.
Crossing the Jordan	"	iii.
The Siege of Jericho	"	vi, 1–25.
The Disobedience of Achan	"	vii.
The Crafty Gibeonites	"	ix, 4–27.
Joshua's Farewell to the People	"	xxiii, xxiv, 14–28.
Judges in Israel	Judges	ii, 11–19.
Deborah, the Mother in Israel; Barak, Jael and Sisera	"	iv.
Song of Deborah	"	v.
The Story of Gideon	"	vi, vii.
Jephthah's Daughter	"	xi, 4–40.
Samson, the Strong Man	"	xvi, 4–31.
The Story of Ruth	Ruth	i, ii, iv, 13–17.
The Birth of Samuel	I Samuel	i, 2–3, 9–11, 19–28.
Hannah's Song of Thanksgiving	"	ii, 1–10.
Samuel's Vision	"	iii.
War with the Philistines and the Ark Taken	"	iv, 1–18.
Return of the Ark	"	vi, vii, 1–2.
The Demand for a King	"	viii.
Saul Chosen King	"	ix, x.

CHAPTER VIII. THE UNITED KINGDOM OF ISRAEL

Story	Book	Reference
Jonathan's Adventure with the Philistines	I Samuel	xiv, 1–46.
Agag and the Amalekites	"	xv.
The Anointing of David	"	xvi, 1–13.
David Plays on the Harp to Saul	"	xvi, 14–23.
David and Goliath	"	xvii, xviii, 5–9.
David and Jonathan	"	xviii, 1–4.
Saul's Jealousy of David	"	xviii, 10–16.
David as an Outlaw	"	xix, 1–18; xx, xxi, 1–9; xxii, 1–19; xxiv, xxvi.

David and the Well at Bethlehem	I Chronicles	xi, 15–19.
Saul's Visit to the Witch of Endor	I Samuel	xxviii, 7–25.
Death of Saul and Jonathan	"	xxxi; II Samuel i, 1–12.
David's Lament for Saul and Jonathan	II Samuel	i, 17–27.
David and Abner	"	ii, 8–12, 17–32.
Death of Abner	"	iii, 17–39.
The Ark Brought to Jerusalem	"	vi, 1–15.
David's Kindness to the Son of Jonathan	"	ix.
David and Uriah the Hittite	"	xi, 2–3, 14–27.
Nathan's Parable	"	xii, 1–10, 13–14.
The Rebellion and Death of Absalom	"	xv, 1–15; xviii, xix, 1–4.
David Numbers the People	"	xxiv, 1–4, 8–25.
David's Charge to Solomon	I Chronicles	xxviii, xxix, 1–25.
Solomon's Choice	I Kings	iii, 4–15.
Solomon's Wisdom	"	iv, 16–28; iv, 29–34.
The Building of the Temple	"	v, vi.
Dedication of the Temple	"	viii, 1–13, 22–30, 54–66.
The Queen of Sheba	"	x, 1–13.
Solomon's Wealth	"	x, 14–29.

CHAPTER IX. REBELLION AND THE DIVISION OF THE KINGDOM

Rebellion against Rehoboam	I Kings	xii, 1–20.

CHAPTER XI. KINGS IN ISRAEL FROM JEROBOAM TO JEHU

Jeroboam and the Sanctuaries at Dan and Bethel	I Kings	xii, 25–33.
Ahab and Naboth's Vineyard	"	xxi, 1–16.
The False Prophets and Micaiah	"	xxii, 1–28.
The Battle of Ramoth-Gilead	"	xxii, 29–40.
Jehu Anointed King	II Kings	ix, 1–7, 11–13.
Jehu's Rebellion and Reign	"	ix, 16–35; x.

CHAPTER XII. THE HEBREW PROPHET

Story	Book	Reference
Elijah Fed by Ravens	I Kings	xvii, 1–7.
Elijah and the Widow's Cruse	"	xvii, 8–24.
The Contest on Mount Carmel	"	xviii.
Elijah Fed by an Angel	"	xix, 1–8.
The Still, Small Voice	"	xix, 9–18.
The Call of Elisha	"	xix, 19–21.
The Chariot of Fire	II Kings	ii, 1–15.
Miracles of Elisha:		
Healing the Water	"	ii, 19–22.
Healing the Poisoned Pottage	"	iv, 38–41.
Making Iron Swim	"	vi, 1–7.
Elisha and the Shunammite	"	iv, 8–37.
Elisha and Naaman the Leper	"	v, 1–27.

CHAPTER XIV. THE KINGDOM OF JUDAH

Story	Book	Reference
Jehoshaphat, King of Judah	II Chronicles	xix.
Rebellion Against Athaliah	II Kings	xi.
Invasion of Sennacherib	"	xviii, 13–37; xix.
Sickness of Hezekiah	Isaiah	xxxviii.
The Vision and Call of Isaiah	"	vi, 1–8.

CHAPTER XV. THE FALL OF JUDAH

Story	Book	Reference
Josiah's Reformation	II Kings	xxii, xxiii, 1–6, 15, 21–28.
Preaching of Jeremiah	Jeremiah	xxvi, 1–15.
Jeremiah and the Roll	"	xxxvi.
Persecution of Jeremiah	"	xxxvii, 11–21; xxxviii.
The Fall of Jerusalem	II Kings	xxiv, xxv, 1–11.

CHAPTER XVI. IN CAPTIVITY

Story	Book	Reference
Daniel in Babylon	Daniel	i, 1–6, 17–21.
The Fiery Furnace	"	iii.
Song of the Three Children	Song of the Three Children (Apocrypha).	
Belshazzar's Feast and the Writing on the Wall	Daniel	v.
Daniel in the Lions' Den	"	vi.

CHAPTER XVII. THE RETURN FROM EXILE

The First Return Under Cyrus . . Ezra i.
Rebuilding the Temple . . . . " iii, vi, 1–12, 16–22.
The Samaritans . . . . " iv.
The Return Under Nehemiah . . . . Nehemiah i, ii.

CHAPTER XVIII. ISRAEL UNDER THE GREEKS AND ROMANS

(From the Apocrypha)

Persecution of the Jews Under Antiochus Epiphanes . . . . I Maccabees i, ii, 29–43.
Judas Maccabæus . . . . " ii, 66; iii, 1–9, 55–60.
Victory of Judas Maccabæus and the Re-dedication of the Temple . . . " iv.

SUGGESTIONS ABOUT BOOKS FOR FURTHER READING

This book has been intended for those who are reading the history of the people of ancient Israel for the first time. The following list is for those older readers of the book who would like to know more about the history and literature of the Bible. It only contains suggestions as to how to begin and is in no way meant to be a full bibliography.

I. COMMENTARIES AND DICTIONARIES, ETC.

James Hastings: *Dictionary of the Bible.*
Gore, Goudge and Guillaume: *A New Commentary on Holy Scripture.*
A. S. Peake: *Commentary on the Bible.*
George A. Barton: *Archæology and the Bible.*

II. SOME GENERAL BOOKS OF REFERENCE

G. A. Smith: *Historical Geography of the Holy Land.*
The Clarendon Bible.
- I. (Not yet published.)
- II. Elliott Binns: *From Moses to Elijah.*
- III. T. H. Robinson: *The Decline and Fall of the Hebrew Kingdoms.*
- IV. W. F. Lofthouse: *Israel After the Exile.*

C. F. Kent: *The Historical Bible.*
- I. *Heroes and Crises of Early Hebrew History.*
- II. *Founders and Rulers of United Israel.*
- III. *Kings and Prophets of Israel and Judah.*
- IV. *Makers and Teachers of Judaism.*

Frank K. Sanders: *History of the Hebrews.*
G. W. Wade: *Old Testament History.*
Norman H. Baynes: *Israel Among the Nations.* (Contains good bibliographies.)
A. W. F. Blunt: *Israel in World History.*
Israel Before Christ.
A. S. Peake: *The People and the Book.*

III. BOOKS ON SPECIAL SUBJECTS

A. W. F. Blunt: *The Prophets of Israel.*
G. A. Smith: *Isaiah.*
The Book of the Twelve Prophets.
Woods and Powell: *The Hebrew Prophets.*
Edwyn Bevan: *Jerusalem Under the High Priests.*
Laurence E. Browne: *From Babylon to Bethlehem.*
Alfred Bertholet: *History of Hebrew Civilization.*
P. C. Sands: *Literary Genius of the Old Testament.*

INDEX

Aaron, 35, 43, 47
Aaron's Rod, 46
Abel, 9 ff.
Abinadab, 68, 80
Abiram, 45
Abishai, 79
Abner, 79
Abraham, call of, 17; and Lot, 18 ff.; and Melchizedek, 20; entertains angels, 20 ff.; sacrifice of Isaac, 22 ff.; purchases Cave of Machpelah, 23; death and burial of, 24
Absalom, 82 ff.
Achan, 53
Adam, 8 ff.
Adoram, 92
Adullam, Cave of, 74 ff.
Agag, 70
Ahab, 104 ff., 126
Ahaz, 128
Ahaziah, 127
Ai, 53
Alexander the Great, 169
Alexandria, 170
Amalekites, 39, 61, 70
Ammonites, 61, 70, 82
Amos, 117 ff.
Antiochus Epiphanes, 173
Ararat, Mount, 12
Ark of Jehovah, 41, 43; taken by the Philistines, 67; returned to Israel, 68; brought to Jerusalem, 80; placed in the Temple, 87
Ark, Noah's, 11 ff.
Asa, 103, 125 ff.
Asahel, 79
Ashdod, 67
Assyria, 1, 123, 128, 138
Athaliah, 104, 126, 127
Atonement, Day of, 166

Baal, 15, 60, 104, 109, 113
Baasha, 103, 126
Babel, Tower of, 12 ff.
Babylon, 1, 138, 146, 151
Balaam, 48
Balak, 48
Barak, 59
Baruch, 141
Bathsheba, 82
Bedouins, 15 ff., 100
Belshazzar, 151 ff.
Ben-hadad, 105, 106, 126
Benjamin, 29
Bethel, 29, 69, 102
Bethlehem, 29, 64, 73, 75
Bethshemesh, 68
Bible, 4
Boaz, 64 ff.
Brazen Serpent, 47
Burning Bush, 35

Cæsarea, 176
Cain, 9 ff., 16
Canaanites, 14 ff.
Captain of the Host, 93
Captivity, 146 ff.
Carmel, Mount, 113
Clothing, Hebrew, 97 ff.
Crafts, Hebrew, 98 ff.
Creation, story of, 7 ff.
Cyrus, 151, 153

Dagon, 67
Damascus, 104, 105, 106, 116
Dan, 102
Daniel, 149, 152
Dathan, 45
David, 65; anointed as King, 73; plays to Saul, 73; slays Goliath, 74; escapes from Saul, 74; in the Cave of Adullam, 74; and the water from Bethlehem, 76; spares Saul's life, 76; laments for Saul and Jonathan, 77 ff.; King of Israel, 79 ff.; death of, 85, 95
Deborah, 59 ff.
Dedication, Feast of, 174
Delilah, 62 ff.

Eden, Garden of, 8 ff.
Edom, 47
Egypt, 1, 104, 138, 142
Egyptians, 36 ff.
Eleazar, 47
Eli, 65, 67
Elijah, denounces Ahab, 106; fed by ravens, 113; on Mount Carmel, 113 ff.; and the still, small voice,

114; and the chariot of fire, 115
Elim, 39
Elisha, 100; has Jehu anointed, 108; and the Shunammite, 115 ff.; heals Naaman, 116
Elkanah, 65, 94
Endor, Witch of, 77
Enoch, 11
Esau, 24, 25, 26, 29
Euphrates, 3, 17
Eve, 8 ff.
Exodus, the, 37, 166
Ezra, 164 ff.

Family, Hebrew, 94
Flood, the, 11 ff.

Gad, 83
Gaza, 63
Genesis, Book of, 6
Gibeonites, 54
Gideon, 60 ff.
Gilgal, 69
Golden Calf, 41 ff.
Goliath, 74
Gomorrah, 21

Hagar, 22
Hannah, 65, 94
Haran, 17, 28
Hebrew, meaning of name, 3
Hebron, 18, 79
Hermon, Mount, 2
Herod the Great, 175 ff.
Herodotus, 129
Heth, Children of, 23
Hezekiah, 129 ff.
High Priests, 43, 165
Hilkiah, 140
Hiram, 86, 87
Hittites, 14, 23
Holy of Holies, 42, 87
Holy Place, 42, 87
Hor, Mount, 47
Hosea, 119 ff., 164
Hoshea, 123
Hospitality, 100
Houses, Hebrew, 97

Isaac, birth of, 21; sacrifice of, 22 ff.; weds Rebekah, 24; deceived by Jacob, 25, 94
Isaiah, 98, 128, 131 ff., 164
Isaiah, Second, 157 ff.
Ishmael, 22
Israel, 29

Jabal, 10
Jacob, 24; tricks Esau, 25; deceives Isaac, 25; Jacob's dream, 26; works for Laban, 27; weds Leah and Rachel, 27; wrestles with the angel, 28 ff.; is called Israel, 29; in Egypt, 32; death and burial of, 32, 94, 96
Jael, 59 ff.
Jehoiada, 127
Jehoram, 104, 126
Jehoshaphat, 104, 106 ff., 126
Jehu, 108 ff., 127
Jephthah, 61
Jephthah's daughter, 61 ff.
Jeremiah, 140, 141 ff., 164
Jericho, 51, 52
Jeroboam, 90, 102 ff.
Jeroboam II, 123
Jerusalem, 80, 93, 96; fall of, 145; rebuilding of, 156 ff.; destruction of, 176
Jesse, 65, 73
Jethro, 40
Jezebel, 104, 105 ff., 108, 114
Jezreel, 1, 61
Joab, 79 ff., 82
Joash, 127
Job, 171
Job, Book of, 16, 100
Jonah, 170
Jonathan, 74; death of, 77; David's lament for, 77 ff.
Jordan, 2, 47, 51, 52
Joseph, and his brothers, 30 ff.; in Egypt, 30; interprets the Pharaoh's dream, 31; and his brothers in Egypt, 31
Joshua, 39, 48; and the conquest of Canaan, 51 ff.
Josiah, 140 ff.
Jubal, 11
Jubilee, 166
Judah, Kingdom of, 125
Judges, 58 ff.
Justice, Hebrew, 56, 95, 100 ff.

Kirjath-jearim, 68, 80
Korah, 45

Laban, 27 ff.
Leah, 27
Lebanon, 86
Lebanon, House of the Forest of, 88
Levites, 43

Lights, Feast of, 174
Lot, 18 ff.

Maccabæus, Judas, 174
Machpelah, Cave of, 23, 32
Mamre, Plain of, 20
Manasseh, 138 ff.
Manna, 39, 46
Medes, 151
Megiddo, 1, 14, 141
Melchizedek, 20
Mercy Seat, 43
Methusaleh, 11
Micaiah, 106 ff.
Midianites, 60
Moab, 47, 48, 64
Moses, birth and education of, 33; kills an Egyptian, 34; and the Burning Bush, 34; and the Pharaoh, 35 ff.; and the Exodus, 36 ff.; and the Ten Commandments, 41; blessing of, 44; strikes the rock for water, 46; death of, 49, 94, 100

Naaman, 116
Naboth's Vineyard, 105
Nadab, 103
Naomi, 64
Nathan, 82
Nazirites, 17, 62
Nebo, 49
Nebuchadnezzar, 145, 149, 154
Nehemiah, 156, 164
Nimrod, 11
Noah, 11 ff.
Noah's Ark, 11
Nob, 74 ff.

Og, King of Bashan, 47
Old Testament, 4, 149
Omri, 103
Orpah, 64

Palestine, land of, 1; climate of, 2
Passover, 36, 166
Pentateuch, 165
Pentecost, 166
Persia, 151
Pharaoh's dreams, 31
Philistines, 62, 67, 69, 70, 73, 75, 77
Phœnicians, 1, 86, 103, 138
Pisgah, 49
Plagues of Egypt, 36
Pompey, 175
Potiphar, 30
Prophets, 111 ff.
Proverbs, 172
Psalms, 80, 130, 139, 148, 154 ff., 157, 159 ff.

Rachel, 27, 29, 94
Rahab, 51
Ramah, 68, 126
Ramoth-gilead, 106, 108
Ramses II, 33
Rebekah, 24, 25, 94
Rechabites, 17
Recorder, 93
Red Sea, 36, 47
Rehoboam, 90 ff.
Ruth, 64 ff.

Sabbath, 165
Salem, 20
Samaria, 96, 102, 103, 123 ff.
Samaritans, 124, 153
Samson, 62 ff.
Samuel, birth of, 66; at Shiloh with Eli, 66; vision and message to Eli, 66; the Judge, 68 ff.; and the Amalekites, 70; and the witch of Endor, 77, 94
Sarah, 21 ff.
Sargon, 123
Saul, anointed as king, 69; and the Amalekites, 70; and David, 73 ff.; and the witch of Endor, 77; death of, 77; lament of David for, 77 ff., 93
Scapegoat, 166
Scribe, 93
Sennacherib, 129, 133
Sheba, Queen of, 89, 94, 98
Shechem, 55, 102
Sheol, 171
Shepherds, 95 ff.
Shiloh, 55, 65, 67
Shunammite, the, 115
Sidon, 87
Sihon, King of the Amorites, 47
Sinai, 40 ff.
Sisera, 59
Slaves, 57 ff., 94 ff.
Sodom, 20, 21
Solomon, named King, 85; wisdom of, 86; builds and dedicates the Temple, 87; other buildings of, 88 ff.; death of, 89, 98
Spies, 44
Synagogue, 172
Syria, 103, 105, 106, 123, 169, 173, 175

Tabernacle, 42 ff., 55, 66, 87
Tabernacles, Feast of, 166
Tell-el-Armarna Letters, 15
Temple, 87 ff., 153 ff.
Ten Commandments, 41
Thebes, 14
Thutmose III, 14
Tiglath-Pileser, 128
Titus, 176
Trade, Hebrew, 86, 99, 104
Tribute, 93
Tubal-Cain, 11
Tyre, 86 ff.

Ur of the Chaldees, 17
Uriah, 82

Wisdom Literature, 172

Zimri, 103, 108

www.ingramcontent.com/pod-product-compliance
Lightning Source LLC
LaVergne TN
LVHW011226080426
835509LV00005B/350

* 9 7 8 1 5 9 7 3 1 3 5 5 1 *